The Education of Three-to-Eight Year Olds in Europe in the Eighties

Willem van der Eyken

A Report Commissioned by the Council of Europe for
the Standing Conference of
European Ministers of Education for their
Twelfth Session, Lisbon, June 1981

and

Edited Extracts of Statements by
Representatives of States Participating in the Conference
Presented to the Twelfth Session

NFER — Nelson

Published by the NFER-Nelson Publishing Company
Darville House, 2 Oxford Road East,
Windsor, Berks. SL4 1DF.

First published 1982
© Council of Europe, 1982
ISBN 0-85633-237-2
Code 8122 02 1

Typeset by CAMBRIAN TYPESETTERS,
Farnborough, Hants

Printed in Great Britain by
Unwin Brothers Limited The Gresham Press Old Woking Surrey
A member of the Staples Printing Group

Contents

The Education of Three-to-Eight Year Olds in Europe in the Eighties

Part I

Acknowledgements

In presenting this personal report, commissioned by the Council of Europe on behalf of the Standing Conference of European Ministers of Education, I would like to acknowledge my indebtedness to the Secretariat of the Conference for support and help in its preparation.

In addition, I received great encouragement and support from the Working Party of the Committee of Senior Officials, as well as individual members of the group. The report also benefited from the services of the Liaison Officers appointed by the member States of the Conference, who provided up-to-date facts and figures, as well as documentation, for my use, and I would wish to register my thanks to them for their help. The list of their names is appended to the report.

Finally, I would like to thank my friends in Belgium, Denmark and Portugal who made my visits to those countries both happy and profitable, and who worked so hard to ensure that I was given every facility to learn about pre- and primary education in their countries.

I hasten to say that, despite all the help that I have been given, none of the views expressed in this paper should in any way be attributed to those who have in this way supported my efforts. The inevitable mistakes, as well as the prejudices and opinions, are mine alone, and must stand as a testimony to the problems of trying to assimilate the complexities of a wide and ever-changing subject.

London, 1981

CHAPTER ONE

Three Childhood Perspectives

Belgium

In May 1980, the city of Antwerp celebrated the centenary of the opening of its first municipal nursery school. Today, for Antwerp as for the rest of Belgium, pre-school facilities are part of a way of life, and although formal entry to the *lagere* or primary school is at six, every child in the city of Antwerp attends a *kleuterschool* or nursery school by the age of five. Indeed, as Table 1.1 shows, the vast majority go to such schools from the age of three or even earlier.

Jan, a three-year-old resident of one of Antwerp's suburbs, comes to his own *kleuterschool* with his father at quarter to nine in the morning. By that time, other children have already been there for more than an hour, having been looked after by a group of nursery assistants. But for Jan's father it is easier to bring him on the way to work, he explains, as he helps his son take off his coat, hang it up on the mobile rack where Jan has his personal coat-peg, and then has a word with Jan's teacher.

The building itself surrounds, on three sides, a pleasant garden where, in good weather, the children romp and play. The whole complex is situated on one floor, so that every classroom has its own exit to the gardens, and through the windows the children can see the birds, trees and play equipment. This particular *kleuterschool* is both large and self-contained; others are attached to primary schools and may be smaller. But they are all based on the same principle of grouping children, with each group having its own, distinctive classroom.

For Jan's family the *kleuterschool* is free, and seen as part of the provision of State education for all Belgian children. Beyond the principle of free access, however, every family is also afforded choice,

2   *The Education of Three-to-Eight Year Olds in Europe*

Table 1.1: Belgium. Percentage of children of relevant age group attending pre- and primary establishments, 1979 – 1980

Age		Pre-school education		Primary (1st stage) schooling		Total
		Boys	Girls	Boys	Girls	
under 3	%	13.5	13.5	–	–	27.1
3 – 4	%	47.9	46.0	–	–	93.9
4 – 5	%	50.6	48.2	–	–	98.8
5 – 6	%	49.2	46.6	1.5	1.6	98.9
6 – 7	%	0.8	0.6	50.3	47.9	99.6
7 – 8	%	0.2	0.1	50.6	48.3	99.2
8 – 9	%	–	–	50.6	48.5	99.1

Source: Ministry of National Education in Netherlands Culture, Brussels, 1980.

both as to how they use the resources, and which particular type of school they want for their child. Jan could have gone to a State school, a municipal one, or a 'free' school operated by a religious community (predominantly Catholic). There are only minimal differences between these various types of institutions, and virtually none between the State and municipal ones. In the denominational *kleuterschools*, there is an additional emphasis on religious instruction, and the staff will have had a more denominational form of teacher training; but beyond that, practice will adhere to the national pattern.

On the door to Jan's classroom, there is a picture of a large apple, the symbol of his group. Group identity is important for the class. There is, first, its own territory, the classroom itself. Then there is the teacher, who is with the children throughout the day, and who remains 'their' teacher for the whole year. In some *kleuterschools*, this concern to maintain an essential continuity of relationship may mean that the teacher will move through the school with her own group, so that she will be with them from the moment they enter, at two-and-a-half years of age, until they pass on to the primary school at six. Jan's school is organized in this way, but he knows that his teacher and his group will remain unchanged throughout the year, and will occupy the same room during that period.

There are some 25 children in the group, and classes can be even larger. In Jan's school, they are divided on an age basis; in other schools, the groups may be composed of more than one age level. But however the divisions are conducted, the teacher has sole charge of her group. Nursery nurses look after the children both before and after the teaching day, and parents are seen at the start and end of that time, or on other occasions. But within the class itself, she is in sole charge. There are few men about: the teachers are all women, and their work is continuous.

The morning begins, very often, with a discussion. It's a useful way to start, because it enables the children to come together quietly, and the teacher to establish control over the large group. The children listen attentively, are involved, answer and ask questions, make comments. They are taking part in what is perhaps the most important aspect of the *kleuterschool*, its concern with language.

Antwerp, like the rest of the country, is a very mixed community. Situated as it is in the Dutch-speaking sector of the country (as opposed to the French-speaking South and the German-speaking East), all education is conducted through the Dutch language. In addition, Antwerp, as one of Europe's largest ports, has its influx of immigrants and migrant workers, with Turks, Moroccans, Spanish and other workers sending their children to the local school. It is one of the main objectives of the *kleuterschool* that no child shall be handicapped in its educational progress by such differences in language, and so the morning is spent on exercises and games that emphasize this aspect of the work.

The children comment on the weather, discuss the coming of spring and what this will mean to the countryside. They work with sounds, playing a form of dominoes with matching sound pictures. They use drawings of animals, making the sounds of the animal portrayed on the flannelboard. Throughout these activities, the philosophy of Ovide Decroly, the eminent Belgian educationist, ensures that experience always precedes abstraction. In his influential writings, Decroly, a student of Dewey, emphasized that the school should, as far as possible, 'educate for life through living' or, in other words, provide direct experience from which children could learn. Secondly, he directed that ideas should be developed from a general view to a more analytic stage and only finally to a stage of synthesis, reflecting the Piagetian model of cognitive development. Finally, he advocated that knowledge should be acquired through a variety of observation, association and expression. In adhering to these principles, the children will not be asked to make the sounds of farm animals until they have visited a zoo or a farm: 'experience must precede abstraction'.

What these experiences might be, and how they may be translated into work in the classroom is broadly set out in the *Werkplan voor opvoedende activiteiten in de kleuterschool* (Programme of educational activities in the nursery school), which every school is given by the Ministry and the municipality. It took ten years to develop the current programme, which contains suggestions for the development of moral and social education, hygiene, road safety, language, motor skills and cognitive development, all focussed on the idea that a good teacher behaves towards her children just as a good parent would. Hence there is no television set in Jan's classroom, or indeed any use of educational broadcasting, for to do so would be to substitute vicarious aids for the reality of experience.

At lunch-time, Jan's mother comes to fetch him home for his midday meal. In this school, three-quarters of the children attend only part-time. Some stay at the school for lunch, others do not. The school is designed for maximum flexibility on the part of the family. Children can stay all day, from seven in the morning until six at night if the parents are both working. Or they can come just for the morning session, or stay for both sessions but go home in the middle of the day. There is even, within the school itself, a quite separate institution called the *peuterschool*, a day centre run and staffed by a different government agency, where children from the age of 18 months to three years are catered for on a sliding scale charge to parents. There is some concern that, even so, there are not enough of such *peuterschools*, or of child-minders and crèches to cater for the demand for all-day care for the very young, and that what exists can be expensive for the individual family. Hence there is a growing pressure on the *kleuterschools*, which are free, to take more and more under-threes into their classes.

How the provision is actually used depends very much on the location. In Jan's school, there is little demand for all-day provision, and of the 146 children only four needed holiday play schemes to help their parents during working hours. But in another *kleuterschool* only a few streets away, half of the 400 children have parents who both work full-time, with a further quarter having mothers on part-time work. In that school more than half the children arrive before eight o'clock, and leave in the evening at about six.

It is, of course, not only these 'extended hours', nor the lack of payment for education, which help working families. On Wednesday afternoons, when most *kleuterschools* are closed, there are play sessions supervised by helpers to care for the children whose parents are not at home, and during the three major school holiday periods, play schemes operate within the schools to cater for these families. This extensive provision enables the family to adjust to new circumstances without affecting the education of its children. As one father explained it:

> My wife does not go out to work at the moment, but she brings the children to school, fetches them at lunch-time, makes them lunch, brings them back again in the afternoon and then fetches them again at four o'clock. She is very busy!
>
> It's good for her to be able to get on with her housework and shopping during the day, so that she can give the children her full attention when they come home. We live in a small apartment, and there isn't much room for the children to play, so they're very much better off here. Anyway, they love coming here – we wouldn't be able to keep them away. But perhaps my wife will decide to get a job, and she is free to make that decision if she wants, without worrying about what will happen to the children.

So the *kleuterschools*, and indeed all pre-school provision which allows parents to make decisions independently of their children's needs, also have the consequence that they offer a freedom of decision-making for the family without creating conflict or guilt. Some teachers are concerned that this freedom has been seized too readily by parents who, they feel, may be abdicating their own parental responsibilities by demanding more and more provision even for the very young. For others, high quality day-care and education are perceived as prerequisites of equality of opportunity for both sexes, and a cornerstone of healthy family life free from oppressive role stereotyping.

After lunch, Jan's teacher gathers her group around her on the rug, as she tells them the story of 'The Curious Bulb'.

> 'It was March, and still very cold, and all the bulbs were under the ground, safe from the weather.'

All the children roll themselves into a ball, acting out the story.

> 'But one bulb wanted to look outside, to see what happened in the great world above. And so he lifted up his head, peeked out from the soil, and saw – the sun! The bulb uncurled itself, and stood up straight, glowing in the warmth.'

Jan stands up on the rug, his arms outstretched, his head back towards an imaginary sun hanging in the sky.

'It's not cold at all!' said the curious bulb to his friends. But just then, some children came past, and saw the solitary flower – and picked it. They took it home, put it in a vase and heralded it as the first sign of the coming spring. In April, when all the other bulbs rose out of the ground, they looked around for their missing friend. But he was nowhere to be seen.

'Ah!' sigh the children.

The teacher brings out a big pile of computer paper, and begins to distribute large sheets of it for the children to draw the story. From a quiet, attentive group the room suddenly bursts into loud life as the children split up into smaller workgroups to draw the story they have just acted out, just 'experienced'. It is Decroly in action: first the experience, then the abstraction; first the impression, then the expression. But it is also the idea of a 'project', one of Decroly's themes, in which an idea is pursued in a number of different forms, through music, painting, sound, movement, words and action. The process controlled and activated by the teacher.

The school itself wants to keep parents involved about what it is doing with the children, and the teacher likes to hear how Jan's family is faring, and how he behaves at home. There are the informal contacts in the corridors before class begins, the contact when parents come to collect their children, the Wednesday afternoons when some parents come to the school to see for themselves what is happening. But there are, too, the parents who are too busy to spend much time in these, inevitably, brief encounters. And then there are the parents whom the school never sees, whose children are brought by relatives, or friends, or older brothers and sisters.

When Jan is nearly six years old, his overall performance in the kleuterschool will be assessed by a team including his teacher, to see how ready he is to transfer to the primary school. What the assessors will be looking at is his maturational level and his social integration, rather than any particular skill or aptitude he may have acquired. If, in their view, he is still immature for his age, they may recommend that he spend another term or more in the pre-school stage, a recommendation which is discussed with the family and can be overturned by the parents. In Jan's school last year, only one child was thought to be unsuitable for transfer at six. Otherwise, Jan and his friends will probably make a visit to his *lagere* school during his final term in *kleuterschool*, to become acquainted with the new regime. Some primary schools conduct joint acitivities with the pre-school to create a harmonious relationship between the two, and others run joint staff ventures. Many pre-school institutions, being attached to primary schools, share common facilities.

Nevertheless, the transition involves both the regime and teacher expectations. The *kleuterschool* does not 'teach' either reading or writing. In the first years of the *lagere* school, however, the children get down to the important business of acquiring both these skills. They are expected to work hard, and with concentration. And for those who at this point begin to fall behind, there are remedial classes which seek to help and support them with their programme of studies.

Spaar Energie (Save Energy), it says in bold letters on the door of the *lagere* school to which Jan is likely to go, reflecting the relationship between the provision of an expensive educational system with the increasingly critical energy crisis for an economy expected to generate such expenditure. The remedial class in the school has its own permanent teacher with her own room, to which children requiring some additional help come for spells of half-an-hour a day. Here the groups are small — perhaps no more than one or two children at a time. The remedial teacher, in consultation with the classroom teacher and headmaster, will devise a special programme for her referrals, and she will see the children every day. The problem may be a relatively minor one, involving only a few visits, or it may take longer to give a child some specific skills that he lacks.

At the end of the year, some of these children may be judged not ready to move on to the next class, and the school may then recommend that they repeat a year. It is a cause of some concern that, despite the provision of generous pre-schooling facilities, such 'repeating' is still prevalent in the *lagere* school, affecting some six per cent of the intake.

This is one of the *drempels* (barriers), which Belgian educational reform is seeking to remove by the creation of the Basis-school, a school which will effectively incorporate the pre-school and *lagere* school elements into a single educational institution covering the years three to eight; what the English system refers to as a first school (three to eleven or three to eight). One of the aims of this reform will be to reduce the gulf that many feel exists at present between the two types of provision, a gulf which some claim is the cause of subsequent educational 'failure'. Another objective is to foster more direct parental involvement through parents' committees working with the staff of the new schools. And a third aim is to bring together the actual educational practice of pre-school and primary school teachers, so that there is a greater continuity between the two forms of schooling.

Effectively, the new Belgian reforms see the educational process as a continuum from the age of three (or two-and-a-half), in which the focus is the child, and the educating agency is a partnership between parents and teachers.

Inevitably, there are questions about such a development. For pre-school teachers, these revolve around two issues: while they are employed on a different basis from their *lagere* school colleagues, they fear that the new schools will swamp the *kleuterschool* element with their more formal ethos, and that the relationship will be an unequal one, in which the demands for skills-training will reach down further and further into the early years. Though the theory is that the philosophy of pre-schooling should suffuse the *lagere* school, they are apprehensive that the process might well work the other way round.

Their second concern is that the generous provision of day-care and early pre-school facilities may have weakened the sense of parental responsibility on which the reforms set such store. They worry that the reforms may be interpreted as a lowering of the formal school starting age, with parents 'handing over' their children to a State system. Is this the way, they ask themselves, to involve parents more meaningfully, or is it really a device which will relieve those parents of their own responsibilities?

How then, do we enhance the development of the child, without alienating the family?

Denmark

'The best school' one of the founders of the Danish Volkschool Movement, Christiaan Kold, once wrote, 'is a house of active citizens'. But in the bustle of downtown Copenhagen, the houses of these active citizens are not always easy to find. In a residential block of flats, on a plot apparently permanently besieged by tinkling trams and motor traffic, and behind a front door that might belong to any residential apartment, there is a fully-fledged *lassoe-gården,* or nursery school, in progress.

The premises were once occupied by an educational toy shop, and were the only ones that a group of local, middle-class parents could find to set up their own community nursery. Today, with State resources, it is staffed by four workers — two men as well as two women — who operate as a cooperative in running the school for some 24 children. In the homely kitchen there is a pot of steaming coffee on the table, around which parents, children and staff gather at any time of the day to talk. The place is open early, but each child, as he arrives, is personally greeted by a member of staff, regardless of how busy they might be with other activities. It is a little ceremony that the staff feel is important for the child and his parents, and it emphasizes that here, every individual counts. For the early arrivals there is breakfast at 8.30 am, but by ten o'clock all the children must have arrived for the day's programme to begin.

The children are subdivided into four 'family groups' of six each; a careful selection of boys and girls, older and younger children, with one member of staff to each group. It is notable that half of these children are growing up in one-parent families, a fact which might explain the stress on the cooperative nature of the nursery, on the sharing of men and women in the child-rearing task, and on the aims of giving the children both responsibility and independence.

Two of the 'family groups' will usually go out in the morning for a visit or walk to the nearby park to play, while the other two groups stay in and work with their teachers on a series of projects or games. Because the school is located in such a busy quarter of the city, there are no surrounding gardens for them to stretch their legs in, and so great stress is placed on these visits: to museums, the airport, the fire station — anywhere that will be of interest to them.

Back from their trip, the children help to lay the tables for lunch, and generally bustle about with a purposeful air, giving the strong impression that they could probably run the place themselves. After lunch, the other two groups clamber into their coats and set off, while the others gather round for a number of stories and 'discussions', talking about what they have heard and seen. At 3.30 pm it is time for drink and some fruit, and half an hour later, parents begin to call for them. Some of the children will stay later, helping to tidy up and prepare for the following morning.

By law, this nursery school is controlled by a Board of Parents, and there are meetings held each month in the parents' own homes with members of staff, quite apart from the informal discussions that take

10   *The Education of Three-to-Eight Year Olds in Europe*

place during the day. The staff themselves also meet formally each month, usually to plan – in some detail – the work that they hope to undertake in the next few weeks. Worksheets are prepared. Visits are organized. Rotas are drawn up. For each child there is a pictorial 'diary' which indicates what the programme for the day is. There is even a schedule for the delightful 'rumpus' room, filled with soft cushions and mattresses, where the children can simply let off steam and hurl themselves around in gay abandon. For children with little opportunity to indulge in violent action, this is inevitably a popular activity, and care has to be taken that everyone gets a turn. The staff believe that by informing the children clearly and organizing the day well, they both avoid disappointment and ensure a measure of controlled activity.

This particular nursery school is not necessarily typical. It is sponsored by a set of parents who originally set it up on their own initiative; who have high expectations of their children, and who consequently insist on being well-informed about the school's activities and their children's progress. The nursery school is financed by the Ministry of Social Affairs and the local authorities, with no parent contributing more than 35 per cent of the cost of the provision, and some, through their circumstances, having it practically free. To the staff, the whole venture has a number of objectives. They see themselves operating as a 'family', though by no means a family-substitute, in which the children develop their own personalities, sense of inquiry and independence, while at the same time seeking to ensure that the parents retain an involvement and a close relationship with their own children's development. What is striking about this particular nursery school is the commitment to pursue both sociological and cognitive goals: to develop intellectually stimulating programmes for the children, in an environment that is based on sharing, self-help and a sense of community.

That sense of community is also apparent elsewhere. At eight o'clock on the first floor of a Copenhagen day nursery, mothers and their young children are having breakfast with the staff of the nursery around a large table laden with cereal packets, coffee cups and plates. A mature student, Gertrud, has brought her three-year-old daughter, Camilla, as she does every working day, and the two of them meet the other families using this particular centre. It is a time to swop stories, talk to the staff, meet other children and generally enjoy a social exchange before Gertrud goes off to her college, and Camilla joins the other children in one of the rooms of the 'family house'.

The day nursery serves 26 families in the neighbourhood, with 40 children and four full-time and one part-time member of staff. There is, in addition, a cook, a caretaker, a secretary and cleaners. An interesting feature of the way the centre is used is that each of the families has a key to the day nursery, and can therefore, independently come in to use the bathroom or the washing facilities over the weekend, when normal classes are not operating. In addition, families can 'book' the centre for private parties, birthdays, weddings and other social functions. Every fortnight there is a communal dinner at the nursery for all the families and their children; a local get together which enables parents to meet each other.

But parents use the day nursery for other purposes as well. There is a sewing class which is held there every week, and in the evenings, groups of parents might meet there to discuss political issues, local problems or simply exchange holiday snapshots.

The day nursery is, then, an important local resource not merely for children, but for their families, many of whom are single themselves, and most of whom, as a result, are working full-time, and not able to afford very expensive accommodation.

Camilla and her friends leave the centre every morning to attend a pre-school class. When school is over, they come back to their day nursery, where they stay until their parents can pick them up. This 'doubling up' of resources is further elaborated by the role of the *fristedet* or leisure centres, which cater for young people up to 14 years of age, and which many children use both before and after school.

As Table 1.2 shows, the variety of provision can be confusing, and is certainly expensive. Because pre-school classes are short — just a few hours — there are occasions when children are moved in fleets of taxis from one type of provision to the next and back again. In a sense, what has happened is that social welfare provision in Denmark, as in many other West European countries, has rather desperately been trying to keep pace with social change and increased electoral demands. In the past decade, while the gross national product rose some 12 per cent, the money spent on day-care facilities has been going up by an enormous 27 per cent. Day-care costs have risen from a mere four per cent of the total welfare budget in 1970, to something nearer ten per cent in 1980.

One of the boosts to this greatly increased expenditure on social services and day-care provision was the Social Assistance Act of 1974, a civilized and highly ambitious piece of legislation which, in 146 clauses, sets out the variety of family support which local authorities ought to

Table 1.2: Denmark.

Type of school	Number of institutions 1978	Number of places	Projected requirement 1984
Day nurseries (0 − 3 years)	508	17,578	69,000 (including private provision)
Kindergartens (3 − 7 years)	2,144	91,719	132,000
Integrated institutions (0 − 14 years)	266	14,575	
Pre-school classes (5 − 6 years)	3,105	55,500	65,000

Source: Press and Cultural Relations Department, Ministry of Foreign Affairs, Denmark, 1979.

provide and which, in Clause 32, states that 'it shall be the duty of the local social welfare committee to supervise the conditions under which children within its area live and to support their parents in the upbringing and care of them'. At least 40 per cent of mothers with young children now work full-time, and another 30 per cent do so part-time, so that support is not only needed, but in itself generates greater expectations. With less opportunities for friends or relatives to look after young children, and accommodation at a premium, the pressure on day-care facilities is growing.

But day-care, however desirable, is not free. Neither are child-minders. Education is. So the pressures to increase provision for the young within the school system itself are great. Indeed, from August 1980 it was mandatory for all local authorities to provide pre-school classes attached to − or within − their primary schools; a move for which many authorities are pleading more time to implement. And a commission is still busy investigating how the pre-school classes can best be integrated into the school system.

At a new, open-plan school in the north of Copenhagen, children aged five and six years of age are being accommodated in one of these pre-school classes. Some 22 of them, with two teachers, are in what is known colloquially as a 'zero class', an unhappy term to differentiate it from the two first stages of primary education, which have traditionally been called Classes One and Two. The pre-school provision is, therefore, an addition to the established pattern of Danish schooling, and the question marks about it focus both on the content of the education, as well as the form of integration within the overall provision.

In the 'zero class', the children are making a large mural. They are painting, drawing, working with clay and dough, cutting out, doing puzzles, and even looking at books. But just round the corner, in Class One, another group of slightly older children are working on a series of word books. Each picture offers a choice of four words, only one of which correctly matches the picture. The teacher, a man, takes them through a number of pages in what is, basically, a reading exercise. Then, the task completed, the children put away their own books in pretty little containers neatly stored on shelves, each child having his own with his name on it. The children of Class One have recently been to a bakery. As he moves around the class, the teacher elicits statements and observations about the visit.

'What was he making?'

'He was making bread.'

'How did he make the bread?'

'He mixed the dough.'

'Yes. And what else did he use?'

As the children clarify their thoughts, and put them into complete sentences, the teacher writes their statements on a board. When a number of statements have been agreed, they can move to the printing set, put together letters that make the words, and print their own story of their visit. The story will be photocopied, so that each child has a copy, and it will then go into the class-book which records a whole year's visits.

Because this is an open-plan school, itself an innovation in Denmark, these Class One children will sometimes join forces with Class Two and 'zero class' children for a common enterprise – for example, the outdoor exhibition on 'Life One Thousand Years Ago' in which all the teachers and children organized their own huts of bark, birch and clay, made fires and cooked food, and generally tried to recapture life as it was lived long ago. But from day to day, the 'zero class' children are on their own, with their own staff, and within the school there is concern that the class should retain the essential pre-school qualities that a nursery school provides.

To maintain continuity, the teachers of the 'zero class' can follow their children into the subsequent classes and in theory they can move right through the school with them (though the problems of doing so are obvious: a good pre-school teacher may have great difficulties when required to teach higher up the school, as the work becomes more differentiated and specialized).

Although Danish children are not held back in their studies in school and there is no public exam until the age of 15, there is concern that about 20 per cent of students seem to need some degree of remedial work in the primary stages of education, despite the provision of pre-school preparation. But is pre-schooling being asked to deliver too many socioeconomic and educational remedies for problems that lie elsewhere? Is the accepted structure of primary education perhaps itself generating problems whose solution is being sought, optimistically, by effectively lowering the starting age of school?

Although every effort is made both by schools and by families to ensure a meaningful dialogue between home and school, with assemblies which families are encouraged to attend, with parental control over school books and equipment, with the occasional 'involvement' of parents as 'stand-ins' on school rotas, there are still some families — mostly, no doubt, middle-class — who believe that they must find alternatives to what they perceive is an erosion of family responsibilities and a steady encroachment of State intervention in family life. The Danes, with their sea-faring tradition and their roots in the land, have a strong, perhaps romantic belief in nurturing self-reliance and independence. For many of them, life in the city is only an interlude before their return to their woodland or lakeland holiday homes, to practice the crafts and the pastimes that spring out of their environment.

That desire both for independence and for a 'return to nature' is tangibly visible at a small homestead on a knoll outside the commuter township of Lynge, about 30 kilometres north of Copenhagen. A small pile of bricks, plastered together and guarded by a wire fence, is symbolic of what the community's 'family house' is all about. These are bricks made by children, fired in their own kiln and cemented together as the foundation of an animal hutch. Nearby, two sheep chew thoughtfully in their paddock, and around the front, small plots of land are being tilled and sown with seed by the families. All these activities — the tending of the land, growing of crops, making of buildings, caring for animals – are part of the range of activities which the 'family house' provides. But above all, the 'family house' is a nursery school.

Every morning, some 20 children and their two teachers come here for sessions that last about three-and-a-half hours. Because they have the complete use of the house, as well as the extensive gardens, the activities range far wider than is possible in the city. Some children begin their day idly hovering on the swings. Others can move to the well-equipped woodwork room, or feed the animals or, as the majority do on a particularly rainy morning, sit around a large table in the main room, working with clay, puzzles and games. There is very little obvious adult direction here, except at milk-time, when both boys and girls are called upon to lay the table (each pupil has made his own plate) and help prepare a morning snack of bread and paté, and a mug of milk. On the table, also made by the children, is a set of candles, which the children light.

The teacher calls for silence. The giggling stops. Gradually the children fall into a prayerful quiet that echoes the world of Rudolph Steiner. As the silence continues, the teacher, very quietly, begins to raise questions, to stimulate a structured, thoughtful discussion, which continues throughout the meal. It is a family occasion – a celebration, as some would describe it, of the communal meal, and the nearest that anyone gets to a religious ceremony.

After the break, the children return to their activities. These may include visits, or working in the garden, or a variety of other ventures. And later, about lunch-time, their parents arrive to take them home again. But in the afternoon, the same premises may be used for a mother-and-toddler group, or for handicapped children, or as a place for school-going children to spend their time before meeting their parents. In the evening, families will use it for meetings, parties, celebrations, to produce the community newspaper or, importantly, for the house committee to meet and discuss the three reports it produces each year to forward to the local authority, which gives it a grant to operate the centre.

Lynge's 'family house' is one local attempt to involve the community in a common enterprise which, at the same time, represents a reaction against uniformity and, more positively, to create a communal sense of purpose, common enterprise and social endeavour. At present, it is fuelled by enthusiasts who have made their homes in this community, and are anxious to see their young children enjoy more than the limits of State provision; who want to create their children's environment for themselves. But the raw fact is that half-an-hour down the railway track lies Copenhagen, where most of the parents actually work.

So how do we balance the family's desire for independence and self-reliance with the need to provide equality of opportunity in a world which is becoming increasingly urbanized and bureaucratized?

Portugal

It is Pedro's sixth birthday. After the summer holidays, he will move to his local primary school, but today he and his mother are celebrating with his friends in one of the pre-fabricated nursery units the Ministry of Education has provided for the local community. There are two classes in each unit, for the older children (five to six) and one for the three-and-four year olds. Both rooms are crowded. There are 25 children in Pedro's class, with only their one teacher to attend to them.

The room itself is small, for resources are scarce. The Ministry has provided the basic structure, and meets the salaries of the two teachers, as well as some equipment, but the community — the children as well as their parents — have furnished it with great ingenuity. The ubiquitous orange boxes that appear in so many guises throughout pre-school institutions in Portugal, have been painted a deep blue and serve as shelves and as storage bins. Old family clothes occupy the dressing-up corner. Potted plants from the gardens make a collection. A colourful rug and soft cushions form a home corner. The children's own toy cars are part of a familiar road display to help with safety instruction. The children's paintings and drawings are hung up on the walls. On a special display all the children have their names and their birthdays, inscribed for all to see.

But today belongs to Pedro. He lives in an industrial estate across the largest suspension bridge in Europe, that leaps the Tagus to the south of Lisbon. His father, a steelworker, cannot be present today, but his mother, who works part-time as a domestic help, has baked a cake for the entire class. All the children, including the younger ones from the adjoining class, come together for the party. Pedro sits in the middle, in front of his cake with its six candles, a study of calm repose as his friends and teachers sing to him, pour out lemonade, clap and cheer.

For Pedro and his friends the *Jardin de Infância*, or nursery school, is a new experience. Although there has existed for many years children's day-care and pre-school provision supported by the Ministry of Social Affairs, as well as a private sector of pre-schooling, the public system of pre-school education was only promulgated by Law No. 5/77 of February 1, 1977; establishing free and non-compulsory nursery schools, to cater for children from three years of age. In 1979-80, there were 334 such nursery schools within the public sector, catering for only some 1.7 per cent of the relevant child population. But for the following year, the aim is to increase this to 4.9 per cent.

Certainly the demand is there. Pedro's mother is convinced of the value of pre-school experiences. 'He seems much more mature, more independent' she observes. 'It will help him when he goes to the primary school.' She has great ambitions for him. 'I would like him to take a university degree . . .' But then she adds, quickly, 'but I also want him to grow up a good boy!'

Pedro has already seen his primary school, and before the end of term he will take some of his own work to his new class and hang it up there, so that he will feel more at home when he begins there. He has already noticed that, in the primary school, the children sit at desks, that they work from books, that there is great stress on learning to read and write.

Pedro will spend the next six years going through the various cycles of compulsory education before moving on, if his parents desire it, to secondary school. He will not have to sit any external examinations during his primary education, but his performance will be assessed at the end of the second, fourth and sixth years and, if he should have fallen behind at these stages, he might be asked to repeat a year. Slow learners who fall behind in this way have a tendency to drop out of the system altogether — failure breeds disillusionment. Primary teacher training focusses on the 'normal' child, and there is at present only one training college in the country which specializes in remedial teaching.

There are other difficulties associated with the primary school system. One of the greatest is the lack of continuity of the teaching staff itself. Every year, some 30 per cent of the younger staff have to re-apply for their jobs, or seek alternative posts in other parts of the country. Allocations are decided from Lisbon, and made on the basis of a teacher's academic attainment in college as well as his practical experience. The overall effect is a discontinuity of staff, and it may well be that Pedro's primary school teacher may leave his school altogether after one year.

Table 1.3: Portugal. Numbers of fully-qualified primary school teachers, with and without tenure

School year	Numbers of 'effective' teachers	Numbers of 'non-effective' teachers	Total	Numbers and percentage of unemployed teachers
1977-78	31.972	15.313	47.285	2.509 (5.3%)
1978-79	30.528	15.609	46.137	1.974 (4.3%)
1979-80 *	34.276	14.327	48.603	972 ** (2.0%)

*   Provisional figures
**   For eleven months

Source: D.G.P. Ministry of Education and Science, Lisbon, 1980.

But the situation is improving. In 1977-78, some five per cent of these young, 'non-effective' teachers (those without tenure), were unemployed at the end of their teaching year. By 1979-80, preliminary figures suggested that the unemployment rate might have fallen below two per cent.

Such uncertainty does not affect Pedro's nursery class. His teacher, like about half her colleagues, is actually trained for primary work rather than nursery teaching, as the decree instigating the training of nursery school staff was only promulgated in 1979. She could apply for a new post if she wished to, but there is no compulsion for her to do so. Though she works with few resources, she enjoys a particularly warm relationship with the community, and especially with the parents of her children, who see in her school a new opportunity for their families. It is said that the major political parties in Portugal — which has had 13 governments and ten Ministers of Education since the revolution of 1974 — have only one uncontestable issue on which they can all agree, and which therefore appears at the head of any coalition agenda. That issue is pre-schooling.

In order to accommodate some of this new provision, primary schools with falling rolls have sometimes given over some of their space to the nursery classes. A new primary school in a working-class area of Lisbon has, on its ground floor, two classes of 25 children each. Such classes benefit from their close liaison with the primary sector, especially in shared resources. A large sand tray, a woodwork bench, tools, writing and painting materials, even rolls of computer paper for drawing have been offered by the school for the younger children. When money and space are short, this form of close interchange is obviously both sensible and cost-effective. But does the grafting of the two go much beyond a lend-lease of equipment?

It is out in the country that the enthusiasm for the fledgling pre-school system is most apparent. Within sight of the majestic, ninth-century Moorish fortress town of Obidos, on a small hill next to a traditional windmill, stands a small, square building. This is Amalia's nursery school. The children from the surrounding villages come here, all 20 of them, from 12.30 in the afternoon until 6 pm, an arrangement made by the community specially to help parents having to take their older children to the far-off primary school. Where else could parents and their local teacher come together to decide the most suitable hours to conduct a nursery class?

Everything, here, is done with and by the parents, local farm workers whose lives revolve around the land. When the children go out for visits into the countryside, they do not have to make special arrangements, as urban children must, to ensure that they will be welcome. Here, at Obidos, they simply ask one of the mothers whether she will be planting potatoes in the field, and the children troop off to help her, to watch the process and to share the experience. Every event in the village is an occasion for the children to participate.

On the wall of the class, the children have drawn the story of 'The Sad Donkey'.

'The sad donkey, all alone, finds two rabbits, and asks them whether he can stay with them. "No, you are too big, you cannot live in our warren," say the rabbits.
Then he meets two ducks. "No, you cannot stay with us, you cannot swim on the water," say the ducks.
Dejected, the donkey moves on, until he meets another donkey. "Please come and stay with me," says his new friend, "and then we can play together in the field".'

There are donkeys in the fields around Obidos, but few horses or cows. So the stories spring from the countryside itself, from the experiences and folklore of the families who live there.

The single room is, in many ways, a microcosm of Portuguese nursery provision. Under a heavy, wooden cross, there is a home corner, with its orange boxes, a nature corner, plants and a table full of games. There is the inevitable road model, with its toy cars, a profusion of bright, small cushions. Across the room, the children's paintings hang like a washline, complete with clothes pegs, and there are large, soft pillows on which the children jump and roll. Because the parents have been able to decide the hours of operation which suit them best, they also have the time to spend in the nursery to be with their children, and to talk to Amalia about them. So the room is full of village gossip, and there is the smell of *bicas* (a small cup of strong black coffee), being brewed in the small space next door.

There is a gaity and spontaneity about Amalia's nursery school which makes it, perhaps, a vision of what the industrialized world has lost, and which it strives to regain. There is no division here between parents and staff, or between the culture of the villages and homes, and the language of the nursery. Amalia hugs the mothers as close friends when they arrive on her doorstep; formality is unknown, interests are common and shared. Amalia lives in the village, and knows all the families intimately. She has a natural authority which enables her to cope with her 20 charges in an easy, unforced way while apparently enjoying herself hugely. Everything is used spontaneously, as it happens.

There are new chicks hatched at one of the farm houses! All the children run off into the countryside, which throbs under a relentless sun, to go and see them. One of the mothers tells of a visitor to the town, so he must be ushered to the nursery class to visit the children. A father takes a day off work, especially to join in the excitement. Someone brings a cake. Everybody must have some. Only the budgerigar, twittering in its cage outside and shaded from the strong light, seems to miss out. He used to fly about the classroom, but kept pecking at the papers, and had to be relegated to the out-of-doors.

It is easy to romanticize on such a pastoral scene, or to contrast it with the more limited opportunities for spontaneous activity that most urban nurseries have. But even here, there are difficulties. Amalia's children have been to visit their neighbouring primary school, and the children are well aware of the next stage of their education. But in general, a gulf exists between the two sectors, with little contact or continuity of method. To the students and staff of the training college at nearby Caldas da Rainha — the site of the first stirrings of the 1974 Revolution — children who have attended such a nursery class are bored with the more didactic approach which they may receive in primary education. Ironically, those who have never been to a nursery school, and who are therefore more likely to accept a more formal approach to teaching, are perhaps better able to adapt to primary schooling. What the students fear is that, as pre-schooling develops in Portugal, primary institutions will be faced with two sets of children – those who have experienced nursery education and those who have missed out. There is a difference of opinion about how these two sets will operate in primary schools. One group sees the nursery children as unruly, too boisterous, as badly behaved and raising problems of 'discipline'. The other group takes a more positive attitude, and welcomes their questing, open and exploratory characters, but admits that such children will pose new problems for teachers, who have not been trained to cope with such lively children, and have, traditionally, been led to expect a strong respect for authority and a quiescent, accepting student population.

This issue, indeed, prompted an experiment in a number of primary schools with a new type of curriculum framework, in which the objectives of the schools were retained, but more time was given over to play. That experiment has since been overtaken by the introduction of a new school system, consisting of two stages or 'phases', each comprising two years. Yet it is perhaps salutary to note that during the course of the experiment, teachers complained that they found it difficult to operate, and parents protested that their children were not being worked hard enough, not 'getting ahead' with what the families regarded as the essentials of school work.

So while Amalia's parents enjoy her nursery school, and while they are quite happy to accept that their children will not learn to read or write at this stage of their young lives, their perceptions and expectations of the primary school are quite different, rooted in the concept of 'school' as a place of work, of being formally taught and instructed. To the staff of the training college at Caldas, there is an inherent contradiction here, and they express a fear that such public perceptions will, in the end, weigh against Amalia's children – that these children will become bored, dispirited and finally, fail to produce their best during the more formal phases of schooling. How, they ask, do we develop the man, without crushing the essential child?

There are, in Portugal, as in other European countries, other agencies which care for young children, and which have, in their institutions, a preponderance of the three-to-six year olds who experience some form of institutional care before moving on to school. Only six kilometres from where Amalia and her children have their class, in Obidos itself, at the very foot of the Moorish castle and surrounded by churches, a clutter of tiny alley-ways, open squares and white walls lit with purple bougainvillaea, there is a house, converted into a day centre, and operated by the community with support from the Ministry of Education. It is in fact a combination of nursery school and day nursery, taking children from as young as two months till six years. One of the five staff (there are 75 children here), is a trained teacher. The nursery school element is free, and there are sliding scale charges for the younger ones.

The children arrive as early as seven in the morning, and they sometimes do not leave until six in the evening, having a meal and a rest within the day centre. The rooms are scrupulously clean, with gay polysterene cut-outs on the walls, cushions and rugs everywhere on the floors, and plenty of play materials about. It is a very feminine world, and there is little space, in such a house, for truly exuberant play or excessive noise. But such centres form an important resource for the very young in Portugal today, and they underline the fact that social trends in Western Europe are being replicated, though in a less dramatic way, in Portugal as well.

In 1970 — the year of the last Census, and hence the most recent national statistics — about half the total female working population was aged 24 years or younger. Overall, the birthrate is declining, but at the same time, women are marrying younger, having their first child within the first year or two of marriage, and divorcing more. (Comissao da Condiçao Feminina. Presidencia do Conselho de Ministros. Lisboa.) But in Portugal, there is an additional factor — the emigration, each year, of thousands of men workers to France, Luxembourg, Germany, Canada and South America, which leaves many women as the sole providers for their families. Hence the demand for day-care, quite apart from the desire for pre-schooling, means an increasing public pressure on scarce resources.

The problem for Portugal is time. As one teacher describes it, 'After the Revolution, everybody's expectations are high. We are struggling with 50 years of neglect. We are short of buildings, of trained staff, of resources of all kinds. Most of all, we lack any kind of tradition of early childhood education.' For politicians, these are demands which are hard to resist. The race is between parental — expressed, notably, as electoral — aspirations and the storm clouds of economic recession. Already, and ominously, the level of unemployment is extremely high, and one of the spurs to higher emigration. But as the country moves to closer relations with Western Europe, towards possible inclusion into an enlarged European Economic Community, it sees in an improved education system a prerequisite for social and economic advance and for personal development.

How can we meet the personal aspirations for families and their children, without crippling the very economy which is expected to enhance their lives? And how do we achieve the full development of the child, without institutionalizing it?

CHAPTER TWO

The End of Certainty

The concept of pre-schooling – the idea that, even before a child enters the formal system of education, he should have enjoyed the company of his peers and the stimulus of new ideas and experiences outside the home – though not new, is nevertheless very recent in its implementation throughout Europe. For some member States, notably Belgium, the Netherlands and France, there has long existed a tradition of extensive provision of such services. But even in these countries, as Table 2.1 shows, advances have been made in the past decade, and for most other countries, the increase in provision has been considerable and very recent. During the Seventies pre-schooling has, in a sense, become an accepted feature of the educational process of European countries.

That, in itself, is a remarkable fact. But in drawing attention to it, we have also to note that the interpretation of that fact varies widely. When we look back at the three childhood scenarios sketched in Chapter One, we can immediately recognize that while these illustrate apparently many common features about both pre-schooling and primary education in three different countries, there are also important variations. Looking at the whole range of European States, this variety becomes even more apparent. Far from presenting a homogeneous group, Table 2.2 summarizes a great diversity among member States both as to the length of their formal school systems (anything from eight to 11 years), the age of starting school (from five to seven-and-a-half) and the length of the period of transition from pre-schooling to primary education (from three months to a year).

Comparative statistical tables sometimes give the impression, however, that the only differences exist *between* countries. This is not so. The greater differences may well exist *within* countries, both in the

Table 2.1: Development of pre-school provision in the Seventies.
Approximate proportions of pre-school children attending both public
and private institutions, by member State *

Member State		1970	1975	1979-80
Austria		32.2	23.2	49.9
Belgium	(3-to-6 year olds)	96.0	96.1	96.2
Cyprus		12.0	16.0	38.0
Denmark	(0-to-6 year olds)	12.0	24.0	44.0 **
	(6-to-7 year olds)	25.0	63.0	90.0
Federal Republic				
of Germany	(3-to-6 year olds)	45.0	70.0	78.0
Finland	(0-to-3 year olds)	7.6	14.6	6.0
	(3-to-6 year olds)			25.0
France	(3-to-6 year olds)	69.7	92.8	97.3
Greece		–	–	–
Iceland	(0.5-to-5 year olds)	–	23.2	32.1
	(6-to-7 year olds)	39.8	86.4	94.3
Ireland	(4 year olds only)	61.0	63.0	53.0 ***
Italy	(3-to-6 year olds)	62.0	66.2	73.3
Liechtenstein		–	–	–
Luxembourg		–	–	–
Malta		7.7	28.5	55.0
Netherlands	(0-to-4 year olds)	–	23.6	34.0
	(4-to-5 year olds)	90.0	95.0	98.0
Norway		–	7.8	13.8 ****
Portugal	(3-to-6 year olds)	2.4	6.8	6.8
Spain	(2-to-5 year olds)	33.5	36.0	41.6
Sweden		–	22.0	22.0 ****
Switzerland	(5-to-6 year olds)	–	60.0	64.0 **
Turkey		–	–	–
England & Wales	(3-to-5 year olds)	20.0	33.0	36.0

*   No distinction has been made in the figures between part-time and
     full-time attendance.
**   As at 1.1.1979
*** Four-year-old pupils in attendance at primary schools
**** In 1977-78

Source: Statistics provided by relevant departments of member States.

types of provision, the philosophy, the practice and the control of
facilities. These variations become even more complex when it is
remembered that the provision is often shared not only by different
agencies within central government, but also by the voluntary sector.
For each member State, there are not only a variety of initiatives – as
Table 2.3 suggests – controlled by different organizations with
different levels of resources, but the provision for differing age groups
varies widely as well. Pre-schooling has come to mean the period,

Table 2.2: Length of pre-school and school attendance in Council of Europe (CCC) member States, 1980

Member State	Pre-school period *	Age of transfer to compulsory education	End of compulsory education	Length of compulsory education
Austria	3 – 6 yrs.	5 yrs.9m – 6 yrs.8m	about 15 yrs.	9 yrs.
Belgium	18m – 2 yrs.6m 2 yrs.6m – 6 yrs.	5 yrs.8m – 6 yrs.8m	14 yrs. **	8 yrs. **
Cyprus	3 yrs. – 5 yrs.6m	5 yrs.6m – 6 yrs.5m	12 – 14 yrs.	6 – 7 yrs.
Denmark	3 yrs. – 7 yrs.6m	6 yrs.9m – 7 yrs.6m	16 yrs.	9 yrs.
Federal Republic of Germany	3 – 6 yrs.	5 yrs.7m – 6 yrs.11m	15 – 16 yrs.	9 – 10 yrs. ***
Finland	3 – 7 yrs.	7 yrs.	16 yrs.	9 yrs.
France	2 yrs. – 6 yrs.6m	5 yrs.9m – 6 yrs.	16 yrs.	10 yrs.
Greece	3 yrs.6m – 5 yrs.6m	5 yrs.6m – 6 yrs.6m	15 yrs.	9 yrs.
Iceland	0.5 yrs. – 6 yrs.8m	6 yrs.8m – 7 yrs.8m	15 yrs.	8 yrs.
Ireland	4 yrs. – 6 yrs.8m	5 yrs.9m – 6 yrs.6m	15 yrs.	9 yrs.
Italy	3 yrs. – 6 yrs.6m	5 yrs.9m – 6yrs.6m	14 yrs.	8 yrs.
Liechtenstein	4 yrs. – 6 yrs.8m	6 – 7 yrs.	15 yrs.	9 yrs.
Luxembourg	4 yrs. – 6 yrs.8m	6 yrs. – 6 yrs.8m	15 yrs.	9 yrs.

Malta	2 yrs. – 4/5 yrs.	6 yrs. ****	16 yrs.	10 yrs.
Netherlands	3 – 6 yrs.	5 yrs.10m – 7 yrs.3m	15 yrs. *****	11 yrs.
Norway	0 – 7 yrs.	6 yrs.8m – 7 yrs.7m	16 yrs.	8 yrs.
Portugal	3 – 6 yrs.	5 yrs.9m – 6 yrs.	12 – 14 yrs.	6 yrs.
Spain	2 yrs. – 5 yrs.8m	5 yrs.8m – 6 yrs.	14 – 15 yrs.	8 – 10 yrs.
Sweden	– – – –	6 yrs.8m – 7 yrs.7m	16 yrs.	9 yrs.
Switzerland	4 – 7 yrs.	6 – 7 yrs.	15 – 16 yrs. **	8 – 9 yrs. **
Turkey	3 – 6 yrs.	6 – 7 yrs.	14 – 15 yrs.	5 – 8 yrs.
United Kingdom	3 – 5 yrs.	4 yrs.6m – 5 yrs.6m	16 yrs.	11 yrs.

*   Ages vary, depending on whether children are allowed to continue in nursery provision 'late' or are admitted to primary education 'early'.

**   In the course of reform. (In Belgium, the compulsory system will cover five to 15 in 1981; five to 16 in 1982, a period of 11 years.)

***   In addition, there are two to three years of compulsory schooling in part-time form, as vocational training.

****   Although education is compulsory by age six years, primary school begins at age five.

***** Plus part-time schooling at 16-17 years.

(*Source*: Statistics provided by relevant department of member States.)

Table 2.3: Number of children under school age, and types and extent of pre-school educational provision in member States

Member State	No. of children aged 0-6 yrs. (000s)	Year	Types of provision	Percentage attending					
				2 yrs.	3 yrs.	4 yrs.	5 yrs.	6 yrs.	
Austria	535	1979	NS	3	30	58	71	school
Belgium	732	1979-80	NS	—	90	97	99	school
Cyprus	45	1979	NS	—	38			school
Denmark	479	1979	DNS, PSC	29	52	58	56	85
Fed. Rep. of Germany	4,228	1978	NS, PSC, DNS	—		75.2		school
Finland	433	1978-79	DNS	9	13	18	22	41
France	5,275	1979-80	NS, NC	33.8	88.0	100	100	school
Greece	994	1979-80	NS	—	—	22	72	school
Iceland	28	1977	DNS, PSC	21	30	23	23	91
Ireland	486	1979-80	PSC	—	1	53	97	school
Italy	5,835	1978-79	NS	—		73.3		school
Liechtenstein	2.4	1976-77	NS	—	—	—	98	99

Luxembourg	29	1977	NS	—	—	76	98	school
Malta	39	1979-80	NS, NC, PSC	8.4	34.3	98		school
Netherlands	1,305	1979	DNS, PSC, etc.	17	42	99	98	school
Norway	410	1977-78	DNS, FDC	6.6	13	18.9	23.4	32.8
Portugal	1,233	1977-78	NS	—	10.5	11.8		14.0
Spain	4,547	1976	DNS, PSC		11.0		62.0	school
Sweden	729	1978	DNS	10.0	13.0	17.0	33.0	98.0
Switzerland	521	1978-79	NS	—	5.0	17.0	58.0	70.0
Turkey	7,271	1979	NS, NC, DNS, PSC	—		7.0		
United Kingdom	4,948	1978-79	NS, NC, PSC	—	20.0	56.0		school

Key to abbreviations:

NS	nursery schools
NC	nursery schools
DNS	day nursery schools
PCS	primary school classes
FDC	family day care

Source: Table based on WOODHEAD, M. *Pre-School Provision in Western Europe.* Background paper to Council of Europe conference, December 1979, DECS/EGT (79) 42, CCC, Strasbourg. Statistics provided by relevant departments of member States.

usually two years, immediately before entering the educational system. By contrast, there is little provision for the very young.

What these developments underline is the existence of a number of unresolved conflicts that face all member States as they move into the Eighties, and into an economic climate that differs markedly from the expansionist post-war period. At the heart of these conflicts are the reasons that have prompted the current expansion of pre-schooling: Has it been provided to assuage popular public demand, and is that demand prompted very largely by the desire of families to have high-quality day-care/education for their children, so that both parents can go out to work? Or is it primarily an earnest concern for the well-being of children themselves? If the latter, does it encompass *all* children, or is it seen primarily as an 'interventionist strategy' whereby intractable problems in the primary school sector can hopefully be overcome by provision at an earlier stage? Indeed, is pre-schooling seen as a separate field of experience for children, or is it perceived as being an earlier, and hence voluntary, stage of the compulsory school system which will gradually evolve, *faute de mieux*, into a lowering of the school starting age?

Madeleine Goutard (EEC, 1980), comments that 'it is significant that the existence of pre-school education is largely justified in relation to the family and school, for reasons such as the need to prepare the child for primary school; for mothers at work; to compensate for poor housing, or small families or shortcomings within the family', and she goes on to suggest that 'the truly positive aspects of the nursery school are often considered unimportant'.

The result of this lack of a coherent basis for provision is that, in many countries, the development of early childhood education is both inadequate, in that it cannot provide for *all* children of the relevant age group, and unevenly distributed, so that, far from offering support for the most disadvantaged, it may actually contribute to the process of social inequality. Lacking a coherent philosophy, lacking above all a well-defined relationship with both the education system and other services, current developments often appear merely to perpetuate a chaotic and disparate collection of resources; some of it offered free by the State, some of it subsidized by local government, but much of it provided by voluntary agencies at fees which make it inaccessible to many poorer families.

Despite the recent expansion which we have seen, the available evidence is that 'the level of expenditure on young children is rather "small" in absolute terms in most member countries' (Psacharopoulos, G., OECD, 1980). Table 2.4 suggests that, despite the fact that nursery education is, as a cost per place, no more expensive than a place in primary education (though various national studies differ quite widely in their estimates), the resources devoted to early childhood education, even in countries with well-developed nursery provision, were only about a third of those spent on primary schooling.

In the Flemish-speaking sector of Belgium, for instance, the 1980 budget for nursery education was 7,208,860,000 Bl.Frs. compared with 21,480,160,000 Bl.Frs. for the primary sector. In terms of cost per place, a child in pre-schooling costs only some three-quarters of the cost per primary school pupil.

So in theory there is room for a more rational allocation of resources within national education budgets. But that is an argument that will cut little ice with primary education systems which are already under economic stress, and which will argue that, as the later comer, pre-schooling should be grateful for what it gets, rather than demanding a larger proportion of a shrinking national budget.

The argument for greater State expenditure on early childhood education is, in any case, unlikely to come from cost benefit analyses, partly because such studies are notoriously difficult to conduct, partly because some of both the inputs and outcomes are not amenable to quantification (parental aspirations, children's pleasure, the relationship between early stimulus and care and subsequent academic attainment or sociability), but also because policy decisions of this kind are more

*Table 2.4: Percentage allocation of educational expenditure on pre-primary and primary sectors * *

Country	Year	Pre-primary %	Primary %
Belgium	1975	6.4	19.7
France	1977	6.3	17.4
Ireland	1975	9.2	27.8
Italy	1975	5.2	31.0
Netherlands	1975	8.7	25.6
United Kingdom	1975	0.5	28.5

* Reported percentages are out of a horizontal sum equal to 100, corresponding to the total educational budget on all school levels.

Source: Psacharopoulos, G., *ibid*., 1980, Table 9, p. 32 amended.

likely to be influenced by electoral demands on democratic governments, than by statistical computations which imply that national
government is some form of rational decision-making process that
depends simply on available data.

All the indications are that public demand will continue to press for
more pre-school provision (for example, Bone, M., 1977). This is not
only because parents increasingly recognize the value of early childhood
education; not only because recent research (for example, Lazar and
Darlington, 1978) suggests that early stimulation may have long-term
effects on cognitive development; not only because women now insist,
rightly, that they are 'more than mothers' and refuse to be trapped into
a permanent child-caring role. The demands will come, rather, from
political pressures demanding full day-care and educational facilities for
families where both parents either already work, or wish to have the
opportunity to do so, in line with current legislation for equal opportunities for both sexes. In addition, the demands will arise because of
complex demographic reasons.

It is common knowledge that women throughout the industrialized
world are giving birth to fewer children, but that they are investing
more heavily in those children they do have. Table 2.5 shows that, with
the single exception of Ireland, a general trend runs through the entire
industrialized world. The birthrate among the combined populations of
Europe, USSR, North America, Australia and Japan is now barely at
replacement level. Sixteen years ago, the average American child had
three brothers or sisters. Today, the chances are that it will have only
one. In Japan recently, a survey showed that 40 per cent of women
wanted no more than two children, and in West Germany, the number
who say they want only one child has increased fivefold between 1974
and 1976.

Throughout the Eighties, potential parents will recognize that
children are both entitled to, and require for their full development, a
considerable investment in time and material resources. Because this
implies both sacrifice and commitment for the family, it has to be
weighed against other, often competing, demands on family resources
and ambitions.

The outcome is surely to be welcomed in a world which has, for too
long, been threatened with Malthusian predictions of doom through
over-crowding. But with smaller numbers come demands for higher
quality of services, and new dangers for children. As one head teacher
explained: 'The lonely child, over-exposed to adult company, exhibits

Table 2.5: *Birthrate per thousand population per annum for certain European countries*

Year	Belg	FRGer	Fr	Irel	Ital	Lux	Neth	UK
1961-1965	16.8	18.1	19.9	21.9	19.2	16.0	20.7	18.4
1966-1970	15.0	16.3	16.9	21.4	18.0	14.1	18.9	17.2
1971	14.6	12.7	17.2	22.7	16.8	13.2	17.2	16.2
1972	14.0	11.4	17.0	22.7	16.3	11.9	16.1	14.9
1973	13.4	10.3	16.5	22.5	16.0	11.0	14.5	13.9
1974	12.7	10.1	15.2	22.3	15.7	11.1	13.7	13.2
1975	12.2	9.7	14.0	21.6	14.8	11.2	13.0	12.5
1976	12.2	9.8	13.6	21.6	13.9	11.0	12.9	12.1
1977	12.4	9.5	14.0	21.4	13.2	11.4	12.5	11.8
Change 1961-6 to 1977	– 4.5	– 8.6	– 5.9	– 0.5	– 6.0	– 4.6	– 8.2	– 6.6
% change 1961-6 to 1977	–26.5	–47.5	–29.6	– 2.3	–31.5	–28.6	–39.7	–35.9

Source: Population Trends, Nos. 8 and 17, Table 1. HMSO, London, 1979.

a surface precocity that masks emotional inexperience. As a result, his parents have unrealistic expectations of him, and at the same time over-protect him. The combination can cripple development.' (Vittachi, A., 1979).

In many other important respects, too, the European family of the Eighties is changing in character. Although there are less children being born, those that do survive live longer and will grow up in families which are less stable. The trend of infant mortality shows not only a decline in all industrially developed countries, but a correspondingly faster decrease in those where it used to be high (Yugoslavia, Spain, Portugal), and moving towards a minimum of around one per cent of live births.

But infant mortality is not evenly distributed throughout member States. The larger the town, the greater the differences between socio-economic groups in terms of infant deaths. Urbanization increases inequalities in death, as it does in life.

Smaller families and longevity are together fundamentally changing the pattern of family life for children in Europe in the Eighties. As Hervé Le Bras (OECD, 1979), in his study of demographic developments in the OECD countries, has pointed out: 'In the middle of the eighteenth century, less than one child in two reached the age of two ... whereas nowadays age differences between children are fairly regular and only increase for the last child. In the past the spread could be very great, if deaths had caused wide age gaps between the surviving children. Some children had already left home before their younger brothers or sisters had even been born. Death forced its presence on all children, whereas today they mostly live to see their great-grandparents die. The idea of death cannot, therefore, be the same in the two cases.' (Op. cit. p. 35.) The same is true for all family members. In France, 42 per cent of children still have all four grandparents when they are born; only one per cent have no grandparents at all by the time they are 20, and half the population have at least two. Indeed, other French data suggests that any individual tends to lose his father through death when he himself is between 30 and 50, and his mother when he is between 40 and 60. For most children in the Eighties, therefore, the family is likely to have many more members than in the past, even though these members may be living far apart from one another, possibly in different countries.

But these trends also mean ageing populations. Table 2.6 represents estimates of the growth of different sectors of the Danish population to

Table 2.6: The proportional development of the Danish population, by age groups, 1970 – 2000

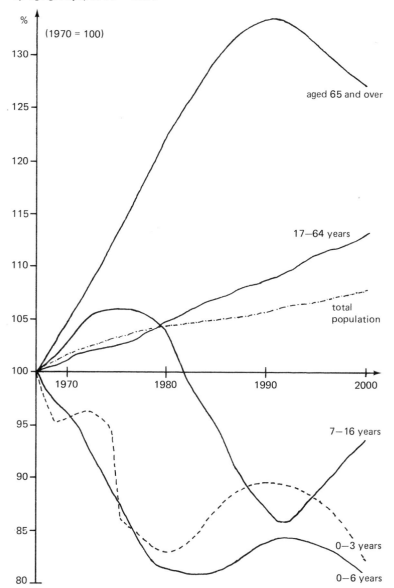

%

(1970 = 100)

aged 65 and over

17–64 years

total population

7–16 years

0–3 years

0–6 years

(Source: Consumption in the Social Sector. Association of local Social Boards. Copenhagen. March, 1980. Figure 6.2, p. 54.)

the year 2000, and gives a dramatic indication of the results of such social changes, with children aged nought to six forming a shrinking proportion of the community, while people aged 65 and over, as a group, dominate society. So while on the one hand parents are likely to continue to have less children, those same children may enjoy the company of an extended social network. As one French commentator has suggested: 'The enlarged family is a concrete fact for the majority of urban households'.

What is equally true for an increasing number of these children is that their lives will pass through a number of different family situations, for in many European countries the divorce rate has doubled since 1970, and in at least two of these (Iceland and Sweden), it has quadrupled between 1950 and 1975. In a major European city like London, nearly one family in three is now a one-parent family, and the number of such families is growing by nearly 8,000 a year. Nationally, there are in England today some 920,000 families, or 12 per cent of the total number, headed by a lone parent. But in Manchester the rate is 24 per cent and in some London boroughs also the rate is much higher: 29 per cent in Hackney and Lambeth, 27 per cent in Hammersmith, 26 per cent in Camden, Kensington and Chelsea.

Moreover, the character of divorce is changing. Until 1960, they took place essentially between couples who had been married for between seven and ten years. Today, divorce shortly after marriage is also growing, and both these types — the 'long' marriage as well as the 'mistaken' marriage — are featured in the divorce statistics. So divorces now include not only first-time marriages, but second and even third marriages. In England and Wales in 1978, ten per cent of all the divorces were between couples where one of the partners had been married before, and another five per cent where both parties had been married previously. So here is another pressure for increased day-care facilities as more families consist of only one — and a working — parent.

But divorce, of course, is often simply the preliminary to re-marriage. About half the people who get divorced in any one year re-marry within the next five years. So what we are experiencing is not a rejection of marriage — paradoxically, more popular than ever — but the fact that European adults in the Eighties have higher aspirations for themselves as individuals, possibly less commitment to lasting unions, less willingness to tolerate incompatibility, and are more prone to see relationships as transient. There is an end to certainty within the marital state.

If we consider these changes together with the fact that European parents have, almost universally in many countries, received formal schooling for much longer periods than their own fathers and mothers and that they are, therefore, more highly educated than parents have been at any one time, we can then begin to see the pressures that underlie demands for more pre-school provision, as well as better day care facilities. Work patterns are changing. Mothers, as well as fathers, seek satisfaction in careers as well as parenting. Poor housing, low incomes, high unemployment, bad working conditions and volatile, unstable family life create stress, but they also generate demands for high quality education, and for better provision generally for children.

The recent OECD report on *Policies for Children* (1980) quoted an interesting French survey which asked people what they would do with their time if the working week was to be reduced to less than 30 hours. Fifty-three per cent replied that they would like to devote more time to their families. But for the 25-to-34 year age group, the concern for the family was even higher: 61 per cent. Indeed, it has been suggested that the family has become the last refuge for people seeking to escape from what they consider an increasingly inhuman, violent, unjust and materialistic society, and that the advent of mass television ('the flickering blue parent', as it has been picturesquely described), has contributed to this isolation of nuclear families, both from wider responsibilities, commitments and relationships.

In such introspective families, it has been argued (notably by Philippe Aries), the child may find himself a prisoner within a claustrophobic family which shuts itself away from outside social contact. 'Nuclear' families can become just that; introspective and isolated.

There are, then, good reasons to believe that in the Eighties, popular pressure on member States to expand and improve early childhood education will grow. That this is not mere speculation can be seen from the note submitted by the Trades Union Advisory Committee to OECD at its intergovernmental conference on policies for children, held in Paris in March, 1980. In that statement, the trades unions put forward a series of recommendations on early childhood and day-care services which included:

'Governments most dramatically increase public monetary support for these programmes . . .'

'Early childhood and day-care services should be developed primarily within the public sector . . .'

'Programmes should conform to strict quality standards . . .'
'All families should have the opportunity to place their children in publicly-run quality programmes. They should be universally available and free of charge . . . '

(CERI/ECE/80.04)

The problem for governments, faced with such demands, is that the other half of the equation, the economy, is not keeping pace with familial aspirations. It is in decline everywhere. The rich man's solution to social problems is no longer an option. We cannot buy ourselves out of trouble. We can only reform.

It is easy, and facile, to rehearse the statistics of economic recession throughout Western Europe in the present decade. Lower growth rates, higher inflation, soaring energy costs have brought with them growing unemployment, increased bankruptcies and demands for punitive fiscal policies. That is the short-term prospect.

In the longer term, European countries are passing through profound technological changes. Fifty years ago, on the river Clyde in Scotland, Britain launched the most advanced piece of naval engineering the world had seen – the 81,237 ton liner Queen Mary. Yet the Queen Mary consumed a gallon of fuel for every ten metres she travelled. It took 78 gallons for her to move through her own length, and 1,218,000 gallons to cross the Atlantic to New York. The basis of the technology on which she was built – cheap, plentiful and readily-available energy – no longer exists, and the consequences of that fact can only be guessed at. Already it has produced at least one tantalizing scenario. The recent report to the President of France by Simon Nora and Alain Minc (1980), predicts the death of the production-based society, with the local workshop replacing the mass-production factory, the branch office replacing the monster conglomerate and an inevitable decrease in the amount of productive work. The difficulty with predictions is that they are nearly always wrong! In 1937, a similar set of predictions overlooked the effects of splitting the atom, the discovery of penicillin and the Second World War! Nevertheless, while predictions may be found wanting, their message may still be relevant – that the current short-term economic recession does not represent a simple hiccup in the inexorable forward movement of growth-oriented societies, but rather the first stage of a longer-term social evolution of more profound change. We may well have reached, as the late Fred Hirsch prophesied, the social limits of growth.

If that is so, then we can deduce that centralized services such as education in the Eighties, far from being able to meet the heavy demands of universal coverage, will instead suffer from increasing shortages of cash flows, and from growing pressures on resources, leading to an inevitable decline in quality and a clash with an electorate demanding better and more direct services. Already it is the case that a reduced birthrate has not notably improved teacher-pupil ratios in schools, but has, rather, led to demands for cuts in teacher training programmes and the closure of 'uneconomic' small schools.

As the values of local communities are threatened by a decline of power at the centre, so there will inevitably arise a clamour from these local groupings, interests and cultural sectors for greater participation, and for more diversification of services to meet local needs. For as Martin Woodhead has pointed out in his recent review (Council for Europe/Longman, 1979), 'the fact is that the European community is pluralist: numerous cultural traditions and values are represented in urban and rural communities'. Moreover, they are, and will become increasingly both multiracial and multi-ethnic. All will demand to be heard and will need to be regarded.

This argument for devolution of centralized services, in which local decision-making, self-help and participation are the natural outcomes, also extends down to the level of the family itself. Dr Doxiades has remarked that 'support for families should have as their aim to enable them to perform their allocated function and not to be replaced'. But what does such support mean, when for many families there is a reluctance to accept their 'allocated function', given that they do not have the resources or the power to implement it?

Centralized bureaucracies cannot have it both ways in the Eighties. They cannot, for example, pass legislation for both parents to have equal opportunities for work, and at the same time claim that 'the family must take an increasing responsibility for its children'. If families are genuinely to contribute to such responsibilities, then they must be given the local resources which enable them actually to do so. To the central question posed by the recent study of Kamerman and Kahn (1980): 'Can adults manage productive roles in the labour force at the same time as they fulfil productive roles with the family — at home?' the answer can only be: if systems change to allow them to do so.

Chapter One provided us with a lyrical example in Amalia's nursery school. What made it possible for parents to be involved was not only the immediacy of the workplace (the fields) to the school itself, but the fact that the parents could decide when the school was open: that the 'tyranny of the system' was not imposed upon them, but that *they* had control of a much-prized local resource. We cannot push this particular example too far. Most people in Europe do not live in such small, rural communties, where such an intimate relationship between services and consumers can be a reality. Yet the principle is relevant. It is that day-care, as well as schooling, is not only negotiated between parents (still, usually, the mother) and a fixed, centralized, bureaucratic system of services and an inscrutable industrial and commerical world which knows nothing about the needs of families, only about 'units of labour'; but that local resources, flexibly planned and community-controlled, operate to support families who negotiate about hours, conditions of work and the use of these resources to their own, and the community's, mutual benefit.

All this exists, *au naturel*, in the case of Amalia's nursery. It would be a curious irony if the energy crisis in the West were to rid us of the 'commuting' syndrome; if families worked and lived locally and if, as a result, we all began to revert to a former life-style, in which work, child-care, home-making and play became, once again, facets of an integrated social existence. All we can do is indicate that powerful forces now exist to drive us in that direction.

CHAPTER THREE

The Needs of the 'Competent Child'[1]

In his study of *The Making of the Modern Family* (1976), Edward Shorter made the point that the great difference between present and past ages lies in the family's 'sense of place'. Instead of seeing themselves as links in a continuous chain bearing its own traditions and history, the modern family often stands alone, without allegiance to the past or a sense of continuity with the future. Whereas in the past people felt that, despite their differences, they belonged essentially to a united community, many modern families exist as largely separate, isolated units. Individualism and self-realization have, in many cases, taken over from community allegiance and collective solidarity.

It is not so for all societies, or even for some groups within European society. But the contrast is perhaps clearly illustrated when one considers a child born into a traditional Arab family, where the event is celebrated as part of a historic pattern, anointed through ritual and sanctified by the community. Here is a pen picture, sketched by Dr Mohammed Sijelmassi (UNESCO, 1979), of such an event:

> A thousand and one practices are put into operation during the pregnancy to favour it, to facilitate the development of the child-to-be and the process of giving birth; offerings are made to the

---

[1] The term 'competent child' has been used to refer to the problem-solving ability of children or, more generally, their capacity for applied intelligence. It is used here to differentiate it from other kinds of children whom we might equally promote, such as 'obedient' children or 'kind' children. Misiti (Council of Europe, 1979), has referred to 'the competent child who constructs her own intelligence', i.e., uses an enhancing environment to learn about her world.

priest, fortune-tellers are asked to find the sex of the child in the cards, vows are made with each prayer and there is no hesitation in sacrificing an animal, if family tradition calls for it. Rare are the women who await delivery with patience and resignation. When the fateful day arrives, the woman is installed in a dark room in which the midwife has prepared a large earthenware tub and clean linen. Upon the approach, the pregnant woman is placed in the tub while the midwife massages her stomach gently and regularly, encouraging her with words and prayers. When the child is born, it is placed on its mother's stomach, in order to prolong contact and allow it to calm down before the midwife severs the umbilical cord.

Again, Sijelmassi draws attention to the important role of the father:

In the Middle East, the baby's father takes a new name which makes reference to that of his son. The whole entourage will from then on call him . . . Abou Mohammed or Abou Ahmed . . . that is to say, Father of Mohammed or Father of Ahmed. In that way it is shown that he takes on importance in the community by the sole fact of having a son who will carry on his name. The genealogical tree is extended by reference to the male child. The latter owes his identity to his father, the former owes his social identity to his son . . . The fact of belonging to a particular family, tribe or clan legitimizes identity.

Here is another sketch, this time from the Far East, quoted by Professor Saparinah Sadli (UNESCO, 1979):

When a woman is pregnant, much attention is given by the immediate community, such as her family, near neighbours, etc., to the new baby. At the seventh month of her pregnancy, a communal ritual is conducted by the family – they make a *slametan*. A similar *slametan* is also held after the birth of the child. The family holds open house for kinsmen and neighbours for five days and five nights. Neighbours and kinsmen from the same part of the village, or kinsmen who live some distance away but feel obliged to appear, will attend at least once at the *slametan*. Usually, women and men will come at different times. During the day the women come; they are served small refreshments and leave a small sum of cash. And during the night, the men come and sit about for the whole night, chatting, singing and playing cards. They are served some snacks, coffee and cigarettes. Thus there is a continuous body of visitors present during these five days and five nights. This is felt to be an important part of the security with which a newborn child is surrounded.

The object of quoting these examples of family and community ritual is not intended to glory in overtly patriarchal, male-dominated cultures, nor even to mourn over the passing of a pastoral idyll. It is to show how, in some societies of a more homogeneous kind than our own, the child enjoys both a personal and also a formalized role and status; cherished not only by its parents for the individual it is, but accepted and honoured by the community as the new member of that society which it also represents. The child enhances the family; the family is enriched by the child, and both child and family are valued by the community. Such communities are fragile in the modern era. A senior official in Thailand was quoted recently as saying: 'There were three columns in our society which were considered unshakeable. The first was our religion, Buddhism; the second the authority of the king and the patriarchal family; and the third our acceptance of fate. Now, all three columns have begun to shake, but the one that shakes the most is the last one. People no longer accept the kind of fate into which they are born without resentment and some actively fight' (Konopka, G., 1979).

But if traditional family patterns are vulnerable in the Third World, they are very much more rare in our own industrialized society. The modern European child, born in the clinical asepticity of a hospital labour ward, often removed from its mother immediately upon birth, has to win recognition, even acceptance, from a society which is often indifferent to it. It is significant that whereas the birth of a child in the Arab or Indonesian context is a celebration of life, the same event in the West is treated as akin to an illness. The family, isolated, reduced in income by the fact that the mother no longer acts as a wage earner, is further separated through over-time, shift-work or travel, so that the mother spends long periods alone, with only her new baby for company. Indeed, it is this remoteness of nuclear or conjugal families, the fact that they are responsible for no one but themselves and to no one but themselves, that marks the modern family (*cf.* Worsley, P., 1977). It has no clearly-bounded or defined kinship network. Rather, it exists in a fluctuating relationship of kin, neighbours, friends and workmates in which 'kin' may be chosen, just as friends are chosen, for particular kinds of help or services. It is relatively 'shallow', genealogically speaking, tending to consist at most of two generations, and it lives in the present, with little reference to any past. Its relationships outside the immediate family circle are reflections and expressions of choice, rather than of firm and unambiguous duty or of historical attachment.

The child who grows up in such a society is segregated at an early age in day nurseries, nursery schools or centres, with only female staff for company, and might well be forgiven for wondering what role, if any, it has in this community[2]. Indeed, it is precisely in order to establish a place within that society – to force, if you like, the assertion of the individual upon the awareness of the larger community – that many young people find themselves in conflict with it, treated both with suspicion and as a threat to an order that is not theirs, into which they are accepted only with reluctance but hardly ever openly welcomed.

Bronfenbrenner (1974), has made much the same point by contrasting the place of the child in Soviet society as compared with the modern American child. In the Russian case, the child has to be reared 'in the collective, by the collective and for the collective'. What does such a phrase mean? It indicates that the individual is brought up to appreciate that his own actions have an importance and relevance outside his own immediate needs, and that his loyalties are, constantly, to the group – the family, the peer group, the Pioneer Corps, and ultimately, to the State. What religious, cultural or political ideologies provide, then, is a 'sense of place'; a sense of belonging to a larger undertaking that denies conflict. To put it more simply, if people are agreed on a common purpose, they can beg to differ about the means of achieving that purpose. But if people have no common purpose – if, indeed, they are encouraged to differ, to individualize – then they are alienated from each other, in a society which may pretend to a certain unity, but where in fact each family is a potential threat to the individual goals of another. Within ideological frameworks, the child and its family can obtain both sanctuary and a pre-ordained identity,

---

[2] For a more detailed, and provocative, discussion of the child's role in modern society, see the Council of Europe study, *Children and Culture*, by Rita Liljestrom (1980).

finding achievement in simple obedience. It is notable, for instance, that Bronfenbrenner quotes one of the Soviet Union's most popular writers in child rearing, I.A. Pechernikova, as placing obedience above all other qualities that the young child should be taught.

European society, by contrast, has undergone considerable changes in its attitude to children. In the seventeenth century, at least in England, one writer could say that 'the new borne babe is full of the stains and pollutions of sin, which it inherits from our first parents through our loins'. So children were swaddled to constrain their way-ward movements, sent out to wet-nurses and, if they belonged to the upper classes, dispatched to various institutions for, being the incarnations of sin that Calvinism depicted them to be, it was important that they should be 'tamed' (*cf.* Badinter, E., 1980). But with the dawn of The Enlightenment, a new social morality pervaded adult attitudes to children, and instead of seeing them as suffused with the Old Adam, they were now depicted, romantically, as the incarnation of an original innocence (Plumb, J.H., 1975).

Children had to be protected from the corruption of man himself, and education was directed towards the social aim of equipping them with accomplishments that would secure gainful employment. This protective concern has had an obverse side throughout the history of childhood within Western societies — the viewing of children as in some way objects of 'property', whether of the State or, more often, of parents. Hence a recent recommendation of the Council of Europe's Parliamentary Assembly which, in its general principle, gives prominence to the fact that 'children must no longer be considered as parent's property'.

As Professor Misiti (Council of Europe, 1979), has observed, the needs of this 'property' were seen until quite recently as almost entirely consisting of medication, harking back to an earlier epoch when infant mortality and morbidity were high and survival was problematic. But as health standards rose and expectations of life began to increase, so there has also been a re-discovery of what Misiti has called, very felici-tously, 'the competent child'; an emphasis away from physical protection and survival and a stress towards the optimization of intellectual development.

It is this optimization with which we are now, as a European society, obsessed, and it is a rearguard action against such cultural obsession which prompts many of the attempts to redress the balance: to emphasize, as Madame Liliane Lurcat (Council of Europe, 1979) has done, the right of children to 'anonymity'; to be oneself, to have a 'private life and one's own psychological identity'. Such attempts, though honourable and even necessary, nevertheless seem likely to fail, for the drive towards the 'competent child' seems at present irreversible. We are in love with high IQs. More than that, the 'competent child' precisely fits the needs of the isolated, genealogically-shallow, conjugal family; competence can be marketed. Competence can be a source of pride. And competence can be an advertisement. Rather than pointing to one's forebears or one's lineage, or finding one's 'sense of place' in a theological or political frame of reference, we point to our 'competent' children, who have gone to university, who have won prizes, who have become legitimized by society through their competence. 'Through our children shall ye know us' might well be the cry of the modern bourgeois family.

It is not beyond possibility that the economic and social pressures sketched in Chapter Two may bring about changes in this current mood, but they are not at present apparent. Quite the reverse. It is not merely that vast educational resources are engaged in promoting the idea of the 'competent child', but that research is making us daily more aware of the potentiality for growth and development of the young child. Not only do we recognize that a baby is developing intellectually from the moment it is born, but that this learning process is reciprocal, that it is actively initiated and stimulated by the child itself, is to some extent controlled by the child, and can be stunted if it receives no adequate response from adults (*cf.* Collis, G.M. and Schaffer, H.R., 1975). What we see is that, far from education being a service which one set, adults, perform for and 'do to' another set, children, the whole process is an interactive and complementary one, in which children prompt and draw attention to their needs and interests, which, if reinforced by sympathetic adult responses, leads to new potentials for intellectual growth.

What are these needs, and how can they best be met? A discussion of 'needs' can easily become confused with a diatribe on 'rights', and the Council of Europe Conference Declaration of 1979 (Appendix A), began with a re-affirmation of this aspect, endorsing the 1959 United Nations Declaration of the Rights of the Child, with its ten principles. The difficulty with 'rights' is that they are easy to confer in the abstract, but difficult and sometimes impossible to realize in practice. Moreover, the 'rights' of children are often inseparable from the 'rights' of adults, families or even whole communities. At the end of the day, 'rights' are enshrined in legislation, together with agreed procedures of redress. They do not exist in the abstract.

But 'needs' are something else, and for the 'competent child' these might be specified as falling into three groups, covering first health, survival and general physical welfare; secondly, as involving a general caring or well-being function; and finally, as one of positive stimulation, concerned with the enhancement of abilities and aptitudes.

It might seem reasonable that a discussion about the education of young children in Europe in the Eighties would subsume the first two categories and hasten on to the third element, but that would be to ignore some harsh realities. Although we have already drawn attention to the general trend for infant mortality rates to decline throughout Europe, there are nevertheless considerable differences between member States as to their provision for child health. Statistics gathered in 1974 and 1975 for fifteen industrialized nations (Wynn, M. and Wynn, W., 1979) showed that whereas only 22 deaths per 100,000 live births from respiratory illness during the first year of life occurred in Sweden, the figure for England and Wales was 219 and for Ireland 343. Similarly, while mortality from enteritis and diarrhoeal diseases during the first year of life in Finland was only 1.6 per 100,000, it was 23 per 100,000 for France, 27 for England and Wales, 41.4 for Scotland and 50.8 for Ireland. These differences are not merely a reflection of variations of national wealth, but rather more of national priorities. Finland, with an economy not unlike that of Ireland, has the second-lowest infant mortality rate in the world, and has achieved what one Minister once claimed was the success of 'actively inducing people to take care of their health'.

Against this, we must weigh the fact that perhaps one child in three living in the rural areas of northern Portugal may be suffering from the effects of malnutrition. Recent reports of a study by Professor Norberto Teixeira Santos (*The Guardian*, August 11, 1980), at the hospital of Sao João in Oporto indicate that possibly 76 out of every 1,000 babies born in Bragança, the main city of this northeast area of the country, do not survive their first year, compared with a European average of 25 per 1,000.

So health cannot be assumed, axiomatically, to arise out of either a well-developed industrialized society nor of a State which happens to find itself at a turning point in its own evolution. It is something that has to be established as a social priority, and it is a prerequisite for 'competence'. Moreover, health has many facets. It is not just a matter of preventing ill-health or even of promoting good health; it is equally an issue of ensuring that the environment is safe for the survival of children.

Table 3.1 shows that in a comparison even between countries of roughly similar levels of industrial development, there can be quite wide variations in the distribution of types of child accident. Why do children under five suffer so many more falls in New Zealand? Why do proportionally more Australian and Swedish children drown? Why do more children die in fires in the United Kingdom?

Simply to ensure survival for the very young is a battle which remains to be won and which, through even a temporary lapse, can so easily be lost. But at least the issues are relatively clear. Better health can be gained — we have the Finnish and Swedish examples. Roads can be made more safe. Children can be taught to swim at a very early age. And in general, Europe can outlaw malnutrition and reduce still further infant mortality.

It is more difficult to tackle the priorities of good care and well-being, the second set of prerequisites for the 'competent' child. Chief among these are good housing and adequate space for children to grow. Here, Europe's record is decidedly patchy, as a visitor to any major

Table 3.1: Percentage distribution of types of accident affecting children aged one — four, in four countries 1972 — 1974

Type of accident	Australia	New Zealand	Sweden	United Kingdom
Transport	37	42	37	36
Poisoning	5	4	1	5
Falls	3	12	6	7
Fire	6	3	6	17
Drowning	34	21	33	16
Other	15	18	16	20
	100	100	100	100

Source: Berfenstam, Ragnar. 'Survival in Childhood — Experiences in Sweden in Childhood Accident Prevention during the last 25 Years'. Address to the International Year of the Child Conference, Australian National University, Canberra, March, 1979. Reproduced in *Social Security*, Canberra, 1979.

European city can testify for himself. As the European Ministers responsible for Family Affairs, in the final communiqué following their meeting in Athens in May, 1979, recorded: 'the principle of equality of opportunity has so far been discussed almost exclusively in connection with education. However, it has been found that school cannot, on its own, adequately fulfil this function . . . The child's future thus depends largely on the family background and environment, and it is therefore mainly by helping family situations that children can be helped.'

The task of providing adequate resources for families to raise their children in environments which are supportive of 'competence' is a challenge which is almost insuperable for communitites faced at the same time with economic recession, and must raise the whole issue of whether advances on the educational front can possibly be expected to produce successful outcomes when inequalities of such known dimensions exist within societies. Indeed, what is the use of sophisticated medication or health advice when conditions for many families are so loaded against their being applied? As Misiti (Council of Europe, 1979, *op.cit.*), put it: 'What is the use of prescribing that the infant's bottle must be sterilized and the infant itself washed every day, if the mother lives in a house with no running water?'

But it is not only the living conditions of many families that are a threat to the 'competence' and well-being of children. Adults themselves are, too. In July 1980, a new Swedish law making it an offence for parents to either smack or in any other way hurt their children became operational. The new law, which was passed by a massive 259 votes to six, not only legislated against the more obvious physical punishment that parents and institutions still regularly inflict on young children, but also forbade 'any punishment that may cause moral or physical pain, even if only slight or momentarily'. In other words, it sought to outlaw psychological punishments like scaring children, threatening them with dire or fantastic consequences for their actions, ostracizing them from the community, locking them up — often alone in dark rooms or corners — or making them look ridiculous in front of others.

The point of new legislation is not by itself to change practice, but rather to create a climate of public opinion, to set a moral tone against which the individual can measure his conduct. What it affords is a strong public affirmation that hitting, threatening or frightening children is wrong. Moreover, such affirmations would appear to have good effect, at least in Sweden. In 1962, against strong teacher union opposition, corporal punishment was banned from Swedish schools. At that time, some 53 per cent of Swedish parents appeared to be in favour of beating children but by 1978, this figure had dropped to 26 per cent.

By contrast, the United Kingdom and Ireland are among European countries where corporal punishment is still officially tolerated and where, as a result, cases occur of even pre-school children, or handicapped children, being beaten. This lack of official disapproval has the effect of sanctifying family violence. In their longitudinal study of some 800 Nottingham families, Drs John and Elizabeth Newson (1976, p. 306), revealed that 75 per cent of all the mothers in their study smacked their four-year-old children at least once a week or more. When the children were seven, verbally competent and when, therefore, many other forms of communication were open to them, 41 per cent of these families were still smacking them as frequently (eight per cent hit their children once a day or more; a third once a week but not as often as once a day). Only a third of the entire sample smacked their seven year olds less than once a month, or not at all. While there were class differences, the practice of smacking was general and substantial for all social groups. And, of course, boys were smacked a good deal more than girls.

So the absence of a strong governmental pressure to abolish such practices provides a social licence for those who believe that such violence on children, if 'benignly' administered, is acceptable behaviour. Coupled with a still firmly-held belief among many communities that children are the personal 'property' of parents — rather than that all parents, natural of otherwise, hold their children in a fostering relationship — such a licence is virtually an invitation to brutalize adult-child relationships.

The third level of prerequisites for the 'competent' child are even more difficult to meet than the previous two, for they are personal and psychological in nature, intangible to the human eye, and yet form the bedrock on which educational attainment is built. We have already drawn attention to the 'sense of place' that the modern family often lacks. For the individual child, too, life often seems purposeless, learning an empty and pointless ritual, and schooling a game that adults have created to keep children out of the way. What gives meaning to educational processes is a personal 'sense of worth', a feeling that the individual counts and has a contribution to make, as well as a social 'sense of effectiveness', a degree of control over our own lives, an ability to make that contribution. We might, just as appropriately, describe the first as a 'sense of self' and the second as a 'sense of belonging' but I shall, following Professor Jacqueline Goodnow (Canberra, 1979, p. 37, *op.cit.*), use the first two terms. Both relate to 'relevance', to a feeling that their existence and involvement is important, that they have something to offer, that their offerings can be effective and will be welcomed. But it is no use talking about 'effective' involvement unless people, including children, are in a position to actually do this; to tackle problems on their own, to take responsibility for their actions, to make genuine choices and decisions, to manipulate their own environments; even, to make their own mistakes (as opposed to being the passive victims of someone else's mistakes!).

It is difficult to illustrate, in a global way, how these two crucial psychological needs that children, as well as adults, have, can be satisfied other than through radical changes in the interpersonal relations that they enjoy with the adult world. Too often such attempts, when initiated by adults, result in a patronizing, romanticized and trivialized concept of what adults think (hope?) children might like. But one example has particular relevance not only for the children of migrant families, but for all children growing up in Europe in a duality of cultures.

How is a child of migrant parents to be given a 'sense of worth' as well as a 'sense of relevance'? Not by denying it its own cultural birthright, its mother tongue or its links with its homeland. Nor by denying it full access to its new, and perhaps chosen, environment, or by permanently ensuring its second-class citizen status in its second home. There is a case for giving such children the opportunity to master their own mother tongue *first*, and for encouraging ethnic minority groups to set up their own pre-school provision, incorporating their own forms of traditional child-rearing practices (or, what the OECD report: *Policies for Children*, 1979, referred to as 'folk practices'). This suggestion, of beginning education in the mother tongue and moving outwards from the home culture to the host culture, is in opposition to the first recommendation made by delegates to the 1976 Council of Europe Symposium on 'The Integration of Migrants' Children into Pre-School Education', held in Berlin (Council of Europe, 1979, p. 146).

Notice, however, that the Symposium was specifically about the 'integration' into existing pre-schooling. But why should children necessarily be integrated at that point, when they have mastered neither their home, nor their host language? That is the concern which is also expressed by a recent report from the consultant to the Council of Europe on intra-European migration, M. François Mariet (Council of Europe, 1980). It is worth quoting M. Mariet's views, not only because they support the idea of initial mother tongue education, but also because they see such a strategy within the wider objective of migrant family needs:

> It would seem, as research has often tended to show, that instruction in the mother language from the pre-school stage is essential to rapid acquisition of the host country's language. As Professor I. Ruoppela has said, commenting on educational experiments with Finnish children in Sweden, 'the better the pupil knows his mother tongue, the better is he prepared for learning a second language'. The main purpose of teaching the mother tongue at this early stage is to forestall semi-competence, which might be described as a relative inability to communicate effectively either in the mother language or in the language of the host country; the maintenance of links with the culture and language of origin thus becomes a matter of the first importance, since it conditions the children's educational and cultural future and determines their 'linguistic security', cultural identity and emotional development.

Current EEC experiments in the United Kingdom, Belgium, Germany and Italy will hopefully shed new light on such efforts to give children growing up within a dual cultural environment the opportunity to gain a 'sense of worth' of their own, as opposed to their host culture, and a 'sense of relevance' within their domestic environments as opposed to the inferiority which so often results from well-meaning attempts at premature integration.

How these issues are resolved remains a challenge for the Eighties. Here it is only possible to suggest that, unless the solutions genuinely take into account the needs — physical as well as psychological — of the children themselves, they will not prove effective solutions. A parallel area of concern is another cultural transformation, when the child moves from its home or pre-school environment, to become a member of the statutory educational system, where we will notice, in the following chapter, that the same issues predominate.

CHAPTER FOUR

The Metamorphosis from Child to Pupil

To give a child a sense of individuality, to give that individuality a status within the community and give its actions purpose are all major aims of both pre-schooling and primary education. As the Belgian Minister responsible for education in the French-speaking sector of the country has charmingly put it: 'Il est indispensable que l'enfant trouve, à l'école, un climat chaleureux dans lequel il se sentira attendu, accepté, compris, aidé, aimé.' Yet the way pre-school institutions and primary schools go about providing such a supportive and enhancing environment are nevertheless very different, and these differences create clashes of style, of priorities and of objectives which may not only prejudice their aim to support and enhance children's development, but might actually be prejudicial to it.

About half the countries surveyed by the Council of Europe in 1975 admitted the existence of 'link problems', or recognized that they were experiencing difficulties of 'continuity' (Woodhead, 1979, p.122). Nearly two-thirds of all member States had professional divisions which were likely to discourage cooperation: divisions of training, status, salary and conditions of work. Many organized pre-schooling through agencies different from those responsible for administering the education service: Sweden, for example, where pre-schooling is the responsibility of the National Board of Health and Welfare. But a study in Sweden in 1979 (Ljungblad, T., Göteborg) showed that the major difference in that country lay between methods of instruction; between, as teachers put it, being 'free' and being 'bound', between being able to follow the interests of the children and needing to meet the requirements of the institution.

What are the effects of these differences, and what are their origins? Over the past decades, European countries have been extremely effective in reducing the pupil-years lost within the education system through children in primary education repeating a year of their schooling either because they failed to achieve an acceptable standard, or through children leaving the system before completing the primary cycle of education.

These two measures, together, make up the elements of 'wastage' as defined by a model reported on in a recent UNESCO study (Paris, 1979). They are both, however, to a large degree 'system determined', in that they are direct functions of how nations operate their education systems, and in Europe in the decade 1965-75 (the period of the UNESCO survey), practically all countries moved towards some measure of 'automatic promotion'; moving children up through the school system year by year, regardless of whether it was felt that they had completely achieved competence at the lower level. The outcome, as Table 4.1 shows, was that this development resulted in a gradual decline in measured 'wastage'. Portugal is a good example. Between 1965 and 1975, the rate of 'wastage' fell from 23-25 per cent down to 11 per cent, brought about by changing the practice of 'repetition' or, as the French say, *redoublement*, to one of 'automatic promotion' in Grades One and Three (the first year of the first two cycles of compulsory education), while retaining a relatively high repetition rate for Grade Two, the second year of the first cycle, at some 20 per cent.

Some countries, like Denmark, Norway, Sweden, Ireland and the United Kingdom moved completely towards 'automatic promotion'. Others, notably Belgium and France, did not, and hence – by definition – repetition rates for these two countries, as Table 4.2 shows, were rather higher. The figures themselves should, however, be treated with some caution (as the UNESCO study itself makes clear), as they were derived from other published sources, rather than from direct evidence. Whatever the actual error contained within the figures may be, however, for our purposes the available statistics make clear the painful fact that the provision of pre-schooling as it is organized in Europe today is, by itself, no guarantee that children will not experience considerable difficulties in their schooling in the primary sector.

Whether the system of 'repetition' is pedagogically desirable is a matter for debate. Its supporters argue that it provides a spur to achievement, that it demands the setting of precise learning goals and hence highlights the need for early remedial attention, and that it maximizes the resources of the teacher, by providing relatively homogeneous groups of children whose attainment is broadly similar. It also suggested

Table 4.1: Percentage of repeaters in primary education (both sexes)

Member State	1965	1966	1967	1968	1969	1970	1971	1972	1973	1974	1975	1976
Austria	6.5	6.3	6.4	5.8	5.6	5.8	5.3	5.0				
Belgium									23.7	23.7	24.0	23.4
France				14.0	13.5	13.2	12.2			9.4	9.2	9.2
Federal Republic of Germany		3.6				3.4	3.4				3.2	3.0
Greece	6.5	6.1	10.2	9.5	8.3	5.1	5.2	4.5	4.0	3.4	2.9	
Italy	11.0	11.0	7.1	5.8	2.7	7.2	5.9	5.3	4.5	3.8	3.0	
Malta	7.3	7.6	6.1	5.1	4.1	1.6	0.9	0.3	0.6	1.0	1.0	1.0
Netherlands						3.1	2.7	2.8	2.8	2.6	2.5	2.8
Portugal	23.4	23.6	23.4	23.9	24.6	25.7	24.9	24.8	24.8	24.5	11.0	

Source: UNESCO, Wastage in Primary Education: A statistical study of trends and patterns in repetition and drop-out. (Table 1, p. 68). Paris, 1979.

Table 4.2: Repetition rates by grade in primary education (both sexes: Belgium and France, 1975)

	Grades					
	1	2	3	4	5	6
Belgium[1]	13.0	20.0	24.3	25.9	27.2	28.0
France	14.3	7.1	6.4	7.0	10.3	–

Source: UNESCO, Wastage in Primary Education: A statistical
study of trends and patterns in repetition and drop-out
(Extract, Table 2, p. 72). Paris, 1979.

that such 'repetition' respects the emotional and psychological differences among children, some of whom may be unready to face the greater demands of subsequent stages of schooling. In Belgium, the reform of the 'basis-school' is aimed at diminishing drastically the percentage of repeaters without moving entirely towards an 'automatic promotion' system.

The advocates of 'automatic promotion' would claim that 'repetition' stigmatizes children from an early age and that such 'labelling' creates as much backwardness and psychological problems as it is supposed to remedy. They would also question the validity of the criteria for judging children at this age, and probably go on to declare that 'repetition', in itself, is an inappropriate way of dealing with learning difficulties.

The point to make here is that all education systems contain within them proportions of children who are struggling, sometimes unsuccessfully, to cope with the curriculum, and that the only difference between countries who have a measurable level of 'wastage' and those who apparently do not is the manner in which these children are identified. In Belgium and France, the children are diagnosed early, and attempts are made to tackle their problems immediately. In other

[1] For the school year 1979-1980, the relevant Belgian figures declined to the following:

	Grades						
	1	2	3	4	5	6	Average
Belgium	9.8	6.6	5.9	5.0	5.7	3.5	6.1

countries, the difficulties are sometimes allowed to accumulate, undiagnosed, partially in the hope that maturational processes will dissolve them, until they eventually emerge at the secondary level of education in high proportions of young people with poor academic achievement. The UNESCO model does not, therefore, permit us to draw any conclusions about the relative success of differing systems in handling 'wastage', and insofar as it may tempt the unwary to superficial judgements, it could be misleading.

But whether so-called 'wastage' is external (revealed by the numbers of children who repeat a year, or drop out), or whether it is internal (the number of children who have learning difficulties, need remedial help, but who are nevertheless promoted through the school), the fact remains that the provision of pre-schooling has not, of itself, offered any tangible key to this problem.

A major study conducted by the Ministry of Education in France in the Valenciennes school district in the early Seventies (Lille, 1975), involving more than 40,000 primary school children, looked at the relationship between a very high local rate of 'repetition' experienced by these children in their primary schools, and the extent to which they had received pre-schooling. Most of the children (52 per cent) had attended nursery schooling for three years or more, but despite this, it was found that roughly a third of the pupils were lagging behind at the end of the first year of compulsory schooling, and almost half were doing so by the end of the fifth year.

Two major points emerged from this study. The first was that the length of pre-schooling did make a positive and marked contribution to their chances of maintaining progress in their subsequent classes, as Table 4.3 shows. Secondly, whereas 4.7 per cent of the children of senior executives were found to have difficulties in primary school, nearly 37 per cent of children of semi-skilled workers and labourers had problems, and this rose to 42 per cent of the children of miners and pensioners.

One further important finding from this study was that the influence of nursery schooling, though important in the first year of primary schooling, disappeared as children went beyond this stage and that, by the fifth year of the primary school, there was very little difference in the length of pre-schooling among those having problems with their school work. Given the very high provision of pre-schooling in France, the authors of the Valenciennes report drew attention to the fact that, despite this, some 32 per cent of the children had to repeat their first

Table 4.3: Duration of pre-schooling and degree of repeating within
primary school (Valenciennes)

	Duration of pre-school experience				
	0 – 6 months	½ – 1 year	1 – 2 years	2 – 3 years	3 – 4 years
No. of children	7,081	8,166	11,271	9,257	1,775
% of children	18.9	21.7	30.0	24.7	4.7
Proportion who repeated classes in primary school	56.2	51.6	44.7	39.7	38.3

Source: Early Childhood Education. Policies for Children – General
Report. CERI/OECD, Paris, 1980.

primary school class. 'One can console oneself by saying that without
nursery schools, it might have been 45 per cent. Depending on whether
you are an optimist or a pessimist, it is the 32 per cent or the 45 per
cent that you will remember.'

The French findings are not an isolated phenomenon. In most highly
industrialized countries with well-developed services and educational
systems, many children have great difficulty in learning the formal skills
of reading, writing and number work. Das has reported (Das, J.P.,
UNESCO, 1979), that at least ten per cent of Canadian elementary
school children develop such difficulties, and many other countries
might put the figure very much higher.

This is particularly disappointing and puzzling when we also note
that most member States have developed, since the war, elaborate
secondary education systems (see Table 2.2), so that compulsory
education in Europe today now ranges from eight to 11 years in length,
with the exception of Cyprus, where it is slightly shorter. Because of
the length of schooling, indeed, many countries have done away with
specific examinations at the end of the primary cycle, so that the
pressure on the primary sector to drill pupils for make-or-break
examinations has largely faded. Now that this pressure has been taken
off primary education, it would seem reasonable that this stage of the
education system is freer to be more flexible, more innovative, more
child-centred and less pressurized to win academic results from its pupils.

Yet despite these important changes, as well as the provision of extensive pre-school facilities, many children continue to 'fail' within the

primary sector, and there is a growing need within primary schools to offer costly and elaborate forms of remedial teaching to a substantial – and some would say, growing – proportion of children diagnosed as having learning difficulties.

Though the 'wastage' figures illustrate that pre-schooling, of itself, is no guarantee that children will not subsequently experience learning difficulties in primary education, that should not be taken as an indictment of the value of pre-schooling, or invalidate its provision. We know – and the Valenciennes research confirms – that pre-schooling does have an effect in the short term. Other evidence now suggests it may also be effective in the long term. Pre-schooling can contribute to a greater rediness and appetite for learning at the primary stage, and Weikart's studies in the United States showed that when children who had enjoyed high quality pre-schooling were followed up into secondary schooling and employment, these children were far ahead of their control colleagues in achievement.

The most recent evidence of this has come from the longitudinal studies arising out of the US Head Start programmes. In that study (Lazar and Darlington, 1978), some 3,000 under-priviledged children who had attended a variety of programmes in the Sixties were followed up between six and ten years later, together with their 'control' groups. The results were impressive. Early education programmes (not just 'pre-schooling' as it is understood in Europe), significantly reduced the number of children assigned to special education classes, the number held back a year in school and increased children's scores on fourth grade mathematics achievement tests. (For a detailed review of this evidence and the US literature, see Raven J., 1981.)

That pre-schooling experiences can, under certain circumstances, have an effect on subsequent academic performance, even at the late secondary stage, is becoming apparent. What is not at all clear is the process involved. It is provocative, for example, that in the Head Start longitudinal study, one of the major findings was that the mothers of children who attended pre-school had higher vocational aspirations for their children than the children had for themselves. Early intervention had bred, among the severely disadvantaged, poor working-class, a group of ambitious parents. And it is this clue which echoes the thought expressed by Uri Bronfenbrenner that:

> It is . . . by taking as its focus neither the child nor the parent, but the parent-child system, that early intervention apparently

achieves its effectiveness and staying power. It is as if the child itself had no way of internalizing the processes which foster its growth, whereas the parent-child system does possess this capability.

(Is Early Intervention Effective?, 1972.)

What this suggests is that the relationship between pre-schooling, primary education and subsequent academic performance is highly complex, and that the common factor may be one that operates on, and is mediated by, the family and, through it, indirectly upon the child. We must be careful, too, not to extrapolate too generally from experiments involving specially-designed intensive pre-school programmes. These programmes moreover are often, in the United States, aimed at a particularly disadvantaged, inner-city population. What we know is that, though pre-schooling in this more general context has value both for itself, and as a preparation for subsequent schooling, it cannot eradicate learning problems and may indeed sometimes contribute to those problems by emphasizing differences in learning styles, in teaching methods and in many other areas.

Because of its serious concern about these issues, the Council of Europe has, in the past decade, paid particular attention to it, both through its symposia in Versailles in 1975 and in Bournemouth in 1977, and its subsequent reports (Council of Europe, 1979).

The discussions suggested, rather like the Swedish report mentioned earlier, that there are considerable and important differences in the ideologies between the pre-school and primary sectors, that children move from a 'child-centred' world in pre-schooling to a more formal mode of teaching in the primary school. Woodhead (*op.cit.,* p.122), drew attention to the differences between administrations, qualifications of teachers, in-service training, conditions of employment of staffs, use of equipment, and many other gaps between the two sectors. In his introduction to the Versailles symposium, the then French Minister of Education, M. René Haby, concluded that the 'search for a solution should not question the specific vocations of the two types of education, which are intended for children at different stages of maturity, but should aim to improve the liaison between their objectives and methods and produce an ever more complete osmosis between the two levels and the teachers working at them'.

The difficulty has therefore become identified principally as one of relationships; as a lack of contact, interchange and continuity between the pre-school and the primary sector, of different groups of teachers, with different traditions and philosophies, working in opposite directions. How could such a division be overcome?

One of the most radical solutions is at present being pursued in both the Netherlands and Belgium, and involves fully integrating the pre-school and primary sectors, and eliminating the gap that has hitherto existed between them by the introduction of the 'basis-school', in which children – voluntarily from the age of about four, and compulsorily from the age of five to six until the age of 12 – move continously through a single, integrated system of education. The fear that such a monolithic approach will mean that primary school methods will swamp pre-school practice is denied by those promulgating the reforms. On the contrary, they argue, it means much greater flexibility for every child. The individual who is not really ready for primary education has the chance to enjoy pre-schooling longer, while the child who is eager to move forward can do so, with the prospect that early mathematics, writing and reading programmes will be available to every child ready to benefit from it.

In the Netherlands, teacher training for pre-school and primary education will be integrated within the new reforms, though the training of staff dealing with children below the pre-school age range, i.e., those with the classic 'caring' function, will still remain separate. In 1979, an enormous effort began to retrain all pre-school and primary school teachers for the new system, and since then several thousand teachers have been offered the opportunity to take part in in-service training programmes. By 1983, when the changes are constituted in law, teacher training will have been amalgamated into a single process. By contrast, in Belgium teacher training of the two sectors will remain, as it is now, different and separate.

These radical changes are being undertaken with an impressive degree of cooperation and involvement by all the parties concerned, and have been accompanied not only with elaborate attempts to inform parents and children, but also efforts to evaluate the changes as they are taking place. As we noted in Chapter One, there are naturally differences of opinion both as to the desirability of such changes and their effectiveness. Nevertheless, the preliminary results of the evaluation teams in both countries have reported a general satisfaction with the new schemes. In the Netherlands scheme, the evaluation report (CEBEON, 1979), which looked at 229 institutions, 77 per cent of which comprised nursery schools and primary schools which were linked to form the new basis-school, reported that these schools had noted many changes taking place within them as a result of the reform. In 87 per cent of the schools, there had been a review of the curriculum and a modification of the way certain subjects were taught. In 83 per cent there had been discussions about changes between the two sets of staff. The schools had shared resources, equipment and working methods.

At the same time, only 35 per cent of the schools reported that they were now paying a greater deal of attention to individual differences between children, and that this was directly attributable to the reform, whereas 41 per cent specifically said that they were not paying more attention to this aspect. Furthermore, only one fifth of the schools said that they now pursued new activities with parents, whereas 60 per cent said that they did not make any changes in this direction (Table 5.4.7.1, p.36, *ibid*.).

The early Belgian evaluation report offers a similar picture. On the positive side, the schools reported that they seemed to be able to identify children with learning difficulties earlier (65 per cent), that they were able to give more individual attention to each child (60 per cent) and that there seemed to be improved relations with parents (61 per cent), an aspect that particularly impressed the school inspectors. On the other hand, the report also stressed that the reforms have not had any effect on reaching parents who have never shown a great deal of collaboration with the education system. Hard-to-reach families remain hard to reach, even with reforms towards *basisonderwijs*. Perhaps even more important, more than a quarter of the respondents to the Belgian survey felt that the new, and largely administrative, changes embodied in the *basisonderwijs* reforms have not really touched the underlying causes of school failure, that the barriers between pre-schooling and primary education have not been sufficiently reduced by the changes (23 per cent), and that children who exhibit learning difficulties are still not receiving sufficient remedial attention in the new system (15 per cent).

We should not place too much emphasis on the preliminary findings of reforms which will require another decade of development before they are fully implemented (Holland does not legally move towards total integration of its pre-schooling and primary education until 1983). But perhaps there are already enough clues as to the ultimate outcomes of such changes for us to postulate that while these, administrative, attempts at integration undoubtedly bring benefits, they may not be going to the heart of the matter.

In particular, they may not be affecting three major areas which concern the whole issue of educational attainment in the primary sector. The first is about staff. The second deals with the content of the pre-school curriculum. The third involves the other, 'horizontal continuity' between the school system and the community.

On the first issue, which we will treat in greater detail in Chapter Six, it is perhaps enough to note that the Council of Europe's CCC symposium on the training of teaching staff engaged in pre-school education in Leyden in 1973 recommended that the levels of general training for both pre-school and primary education should be similar. Woodhead, reporting on the Council's survey (Council of Europe, 1979, p.125), found that pre-school teachers were often recruited younger and with lower entry qualifications, had shorter training, and enjoyed lower status in the eyes of their primary school colleagues, sometimes reflected in lower salaries and longer hours of work. 'These divisions stand in the way of cooperation or exchange on an equal status between the professionals responsible for each sector of education.' Where such divisions exist, and continue, genuine cooperation and interaction and successful integration of the two sectors will not succeed beyond the superficial level of an exchange of information.

The second point is just as fundamental. It has often been pointed out that the transition from pre-school to primary education reflects a movement from childhood to pupildom, from a 'child-centred' philosophy to a 'school-oriented' philosophy; from a domain of concrete experiences to a world of more generalizable concepts. There is some evidence that this transition, in many countries, has become institutionalized to the point where, as we observed in Chapter One, some activities seemed to be omitted, the teaching of which have been appropriated by the primary sector. Instead, the pre-school curriculum has become not only limited in scope, but 'romanticized', encapsulating a fantasy of childhood innocence such as adults tend to nourish. The fact that pre-school provision is dominated by women, for reasons which are well understood but which will only change if conditions of service alter, probably does not help this situation. Yet Chapter One also offered examples of curricula which were more realistic, and which took full note of children's learning capacities as well as for their need to be involved in the world outside their own institutions.

One particularly interesting example of such attempts to re-write the pre-school curriculum is contained in the pre-school project of the Deutsches Jugendinstitut (OECD/CERI, 1978). The research focused on developing a series of units of work, arising out of children's experiences and interests, and involving photographs, films, tape recordings and material from the children's own homes, as well as discussions with people in the community, around subjects such as 'children in hospital', 'getting lost in the city', 'children of foreign workers' and 'about fairy tales'. To use this new material placed new demands on the pre-school teacher, and so a second phase of this research, taking place in 250 kindergartens throughout West Germany, is now under way.

A programme such as that being developed by the Deutsches Jugendinstitut recognizes that children are not only in need of care and nurturance, of love and affection, but that their youth should not preclude them from a host of experiences outside the domain of their own pre-school institutions and should, in addition, develop and stimulate their abilities, rather than restricting these to a pre-arranged set of pre-learning activities cocooned in a romanticized setting. As Rick Heber, the American researcher who worked on an educational programme with disadvantaged black families, observed:

> What most astounded us was the great possibilities all children have for intellectual growth. All of us who are concerned with this programme firmly believe that every child (and not just those who come from a disadvantaged milieu) is capable of learning much more than he learns today, and obtaining much better intellectual and scholastic results. Children are born with an immense capacity, and we adults do nothing but continually take something away from this initial potential (Interview given to journalist Piero Angela in *Da zero a tre anni*. La Nascita Della Mente. (ed) Garzanti, Milan, 1973).

To put it bluntly: three-year-old children can learn to swim in a matter of weeks. Most of them can learn to type in a matter of hours. They can play with telephones, calculators and even mini-computers, and love doing so. The trouble is that their teachers can often do none of these things! We need to optimize the curriculum of pre-schooling so that the child may enjoy a natural right to develop his curiosity and talents to the best of his ability, regardless of the administrative constraints which at present hinder development.

The third area which we have suggested will have to be tackled if primary education is truly to build upon the promise of pre-schooling is more diffuse, and we will approach it by considering some evidence from the British primary school system.

In a recent survey by school inspectors in England, who looked at the work of 542 schools, comprising 1,200 classes throughout the country (DES, *Primary Education in England*, 1978), an examination was made of the general attainment of children at reading and mathematics, and of the variables affecting performance. What is clear from that survey is that there was one, over-riding factor: the locality of the school. Neither the size of the class (the teacher-pupil ratio), nor the organization of the schools (into separate infant and junior classes, or combinations of both), had much influence on performance. Nor, seemingly, did the teaching styles or even qualifications of the staff.

The inspectors divided the schools they surveyed into three groups – 'inner city', (three-fifths of which were in areas of marked social difficulty); 'rural', (with only one-tenth of them in areas of social difficulty); and 'other urban' (which had a less favourable pupil-teacher ratio, hence a larger average class size, but tended to be rather better equipped).

Levels of performance in reading and mathematics were tested in all three types of schools at 9 and 11 years of age. The outcomes, represented by the average scores attained by the pupils, are shown in Table 4.4.

The figures indicate that reading scores for nine- and 11-year-old children as well as for mathematics among 11 year olds was significantly lower for classes in 'inner city' schools, despite the fact that staff ratios were largely the same. Seven out of ten 'inner city' schools had children – often a substantial number – with special English language needs, whereas only four out of ten 'other urban' schools had such children, and only one in ten 'rural' schools reported having such

Table 4.4: Levels of performance in reading and mathematics

Locality	Reading test (9 year olds)	Reading test (11 year olds)	Mathematics test (11 year olds)
Inner city	17.9	27.9	24.5
Other urban	20.3	32.0	28.3
Rural	20.7	30.6	28.3

Source: *Primary Education in England.* DES, 1978, HMSO.

children. Half of the 'inner city' schools had three per cent or more of children whose first language was not English, compared with one out of five in 'other urban' classes. There were virtually no schools with these proportions in rural areas.

Many other studies, moreover, have shown that this level of 'internal wastage' is strongly related to class. Reading, 'the key to much of the learning that will come later and to the possibility of independent study' (DES, Bullock Report, 1975) is a skill which, in general, has improved over time in English primary schools. Yet within that overall trend, there are disturbing signs that children with fathers in manual or semi-skilled work have dropped further behind in the past decade. The National Child Development Study (Davie, R., Butler, N., Goldstein, H., 1972) revealed that 48 per cent of children from social class V were 'poor readers' at seven years of age, compared with eight per cent in social class I. Other studies have shown that these correlations relate

Table 4.5: Proportion of contribution of parental attitudes, home circumstances and state of school to variation in educational performance (United Kingdom)

		Between schools		
	Infants (5 – 7)	Lower juniors (8 – 9)	Top juniors (10 – 11)	All children
Parental attitudes	24	20	39	28
Home circumstances	16	25	17	20
State of school	20	22	12	17
Unexplained*	40	33	32	35
	100	100	100	100
		Within schools		
Parental attitudes	16	15	29	20
Home circumstances	9	9	7	9
State of school	14	15	22	17
Unexplained*	61	61	42	54
	100	100	100	100

* The unexplained variance is due to differences between children not covered by the variables and to errors of measurement. That so much variation *is* explained is due in part to the comparatively simple nature of the criterion variable, a reading comprehension test.

Source: Department of Education and Science. Plowden Report. *Children and their Primary Schools.* Vol. 1, p. 33, 1967, HMSO.

not only to reading. Performance, in general, is strongly associated with three factors within the English system – parental attitudes, home circumstances and the characteristics of the school itself.

It is important to note from Table 4.5, which comes from the Plowden Report, that parental attitudes are not only, in general, the most important variable leading to successful performance but that this influence grows: that whereas the attitudes of parents, and family circumstances explain 40 per cent of the variation in performance between schools at the 'infant' stage, it is 45 per cent at the 'lower junior' level and up to 56 per cent for 'top juniors'. It is speculation whether this growing influence of the home in the performance of children may account for the 'sleeper' effect that has been noticed in recent follow-up studies on the effectiveness of Head Start programmes in the United States (Lazar *et al., op.cit.*). What is not in question is that the effectiveness of primary schooling is closely bound up with the backgrounds of the children themselves, and that the causes of 'internal wastage' are, equally, rooted in those backgrounds.

So in the metamorphosis of the child from playful infant to learner pupil, the support and involvement of the family and community act either as a spur or as a brake to progress. It is in the light of this factor that the preliminary evaluation reports of the Dutch and Belgian reforms should be read, when they draw attention to the fact that work with parents has not been a priority, or when they report that 'hard-to-reach' families remain so in the new forms of primary provision.

But how, then, should we so alter our primary systems as to attack this important area? How can we work 'with, and through' the family?

CHAPTER FIVE

Working 'with, and through' the Family

In the Declaration agreed by participants at the Council of Europe's 1979 Conference on 'From birth to eight: young children in European society in the 1980s' (see Appendix A), one of the major issues on which there was agreement was that:

> 'All services with a contribution to make to the development of young children should work with, and through, the family to provide continuity of experience for the child.'

In itself, this was a powerful and significant re-affirmation of the central importance of the family in the 1980s. But is also represented a growing awareness that the process of professionalizing knowledge, of institutionalizing social issues and of segregating — in this particular case — young children from the community in which they live has had some less welcome consequences. The creation of powerful professional groups in the fields of health, social work and education has not only threatened to disenfranchise the family from control over some of the major developmental aspects of its own children, but has actually removed from the general population areas of knowledge and action which at one time were part of its culture.

This is well illustrated by Misiti (1979, *op.cit.*), who observed, in a medical context, that:

> Mothers are no longer experts. The sources of their knowledge are denied, and being a good mother now means applying the rules prescribed by the doctor-paediatrician expert on the basis of a 'scientific' knowledge of the child.
>
> Giving the mother tables for the infant's meal or sleep means

prescribing that the mother is not to observe the child, and not to interpret its needs on the basis of the specific signals 'her' child emits on various occasions. Instead, she is supposed to ensure that the child adapts to the average needs of a population, rather than to its own individuality.

The Council of Europe Conference Declaration posed the question as to whether professionalism of infancy and childhood has gone too far. As Martin Woodhead has observed (Council of Europe, 1977), unilateral attempts by schools to intervene and replace the learning experiences of the home are not only 'a denial, a negation of the values, attitudes and experiences of the home'. They are also a recognition that such unilateral intervention actually does not work. The dilemma for policy-makers is acute. By standardizing the primary school programme, they have not been able to eradicate the inherent differences which children bring with them into the classroom, and which result in widely differing levels of scholastic attainment. And in their ambition to ameliorate these differences through providing extensive pre-school services, they have found that the results not only do not live up to their expectations, but that they are almost as variable as before.

The problem is how to achieve a high quality of education which will reduce, if not eliminate, the concept of failure and deliver a personal educational service to each child — allowing for a divergence of individual interest and ability — without resorting to crude, across-the-board examinations or a battery of testing which will inevitably have the effect of limiting the broad range of learning possibilities open to the child; how are such goals to be achieved with a qualified teaching staff which, in most instances, in practice means one teacher to a group of perhaps 25 to 30 children.

The implication, backed by considerable experience in many countries, is that it cannot be achieved by schools acting alone, in isolation from the community at large; that it needs the active support and cooperation of parents and the wide community if it is to succeed in its aims. We arrive, therefore, at a quite different formulation of the issue: far from families having to 'fall in line' with the demands of professional institutions, we have to recognize that those institutions are, to some degree, unable to fulfil their functions without the active support, cooperation and involvement of the communities they seek to serve. The question now is: what form should this support and cooperation take?

In a survey of 549 pre-school student teachers conducted by the Kohnstamm Institute in Amsterdam in 1977, students were asked their views about the relative importance of various stated reasons for involving parents, and families generally, in the pre-school education of their children. Their responses are given in Table 5.1.

When the students were asked to say which of these reasons they felt to be of greatest importance, No. 5 was placed first, with 76 per cent of the students making it one of their three most important reasons, and No. 2 was placed second, with 68 per cent popularity. These two reasons were by far the dominant ones for the students, with No. 4, the third most popular category, receiving only 40 per cent of votes. In discussing these findings, the author concluded that there were three *models* of pre-schooling that emerged from the perceptions of the students.

The first, a 'child-care' model, was mainly designed to provide a comfortable and happy environment for the children themselves, and placed very little importance on parental involvement. The second, or 'structured' model, tried to fit the children into a pro formulated programme of work and play, and therefore found it important to learn from parents about the children, in order to ensure that they will be accommodated within the structure. The third, or 'open-ended' model, sought to adapt the work of the nursery school to the perceived needs of the child and his family, and therefore saw the parental role as vital in developing its own work with the children.

These models are, of course, shaped by what teachers and student-teachers think about parents and families, and when the Dutch study asked about this, it emerged that 49 per cent of the students felt that parents were not knowledgeable enough about their children to make judgements on their progress, or to provide useful commentaries on the work of the nursery school. In particular, they felt that parents did not know enough about the pedagogical aspect of the school.

Although it is both difficult and dangerous to generalize from a single study, its findings do, on the face of it, seem to reflect quite accurately the views of many teachers in member States about the nature of parental participation. That is to say, many teachers and institutions consider that the major function of relationships between parents and schools should be one of *institution-based communication and cooperation*. That model is perhaps best personified by the Dutch and Belgian programmes – the *basisonderwijs*, in the Netherlands, and the *vernieuwd lager onderwijs* or VLO in Belgium – both of which we discussed in Chapter Four.

Table 5.1: Relative importance of reasons given for parental participation*

Reasons	Important %	*Not important %
1 Parents enable staff to have more time to spend with children	47	12
2 To give parents greater insight into the activities of the nursery school	82	1
3 Parents can give staff great help with repairing toys, collecting jumble etc.	54	14
4 To enable the nursery school to relate more closely to the child's family	52	11
5 To understand individual children better by obtaining background information from their parents	86	2
6 To come to an agreement with parents about a programme to suit their children	38	20
7 Children cannot be given meaningful help without information from their parents about them, and about the learning and play resources within their community	45	11
8 To come together with parents to press for better facilities and resources for the nursery school	51	17

* Survey of 549 pre-school student teachers.
** The category 'Of some importance' has been left out.

Source: Janssen-Vos, F. Contacten met ouders: bijzaak of noodzaak? Jeugd in School en Wereld, 1977, pp. 358–366.

To explain the changes to parents, each Dutch and Belgian family was sent well-designed brochures emphasizing the importance of their role and encouraging them to feel 'part of the school community'. This involvement was to be achieved through direct contact with teachers, by participation through parents' committees, by parents' evenings and, interestingly enough, by inviting parents into the classrooms not only to observe but also to help.

The problem with such an approach is that, while it may suit large numbers of families for whom there is no intrinsic conflict between the school system and home, it may be less inviting — even threatening — to those very families for whom the formal education system represents an authoritarian, hierarchical establishment, unhappy memories of which they retain from their own childhood. The very fact that many teachers consider parents to be, in some sense, 'inadequate' in their understanding of pedagogic practice, as revealed in the Dutch survey, adds to the feeling some parents have of an unequal relationship between the institution, backed by all the powers of the State and local government, and the individual family.

Such relationships can be confidence-sapping, and there is growing evidence that confidence and a sense of 'control' are prerequisites to scholastic achievement. In a study of black and white children in Montreal, Das (UNESCO, 1979, *ob.cit.,*), and his colleagues could not find the usual (i.e. American) pattern of backwardness among the blacks in cognitive achievement. 'The black parents came out as high on "locus of control" as the whites; they believed that they were in control of their destiny. Probably such an attitude of internal control is part of a favourable self-concept that the blacks in Montreal have, the effects of which spill over to the cognitive performance of their children.' In describing these studies, Das went on to suggest that one should do everything 'that will enhance the child's sense of control, his feeling of self-worth'.

This sense of 'self-worth' has also been found effective with children. An educational psychologist in Somerset, England, has found that poor readers can be significantly helped, not by giving them additional tuition, but simply by offering them someone who will take a personal interest in them; a counsellor (Lawrence, D. and Blagg, N., 1974).

That this enhancement of the relevance of both the child and his family in the learning process is not simply a fashionable cry to democratize the educational system is shown by a recent piece of research and innovation conducted in the London Borough of Haringey (Tizard, J., Hewison, J. and Schofield, W.N., 1980). The parents of two school classes of children aged seven to eight were encouraged to help by hearing them read every other evening. The children brought home appropriate reading materials from the school, but no special equipment or reading schemes were involved. At the end of two years, these working-class, multiracial children had reading ages which were as good as the average for their age across the country, a surprising result for children in an inner-city, working-class area. A year later, they had retained their skill and were progressing well.

In contrast, a control group of children of the same age and background, who had extra help from a teacher within the school itself, were not doing quite so well, and two control groups which learned to read only with their classroom teacher, and without any special parental involvement were also, on average, reading less well.

In this study, it is important to stress that *all* the children in the experimental group seemed to gain from the experience of having parental support in the home: not merely those most in need of it, and that *virtually all* the parents, and not just those already in favour of such home support, were able to provide help for their children. In other words, many parents who might appear diffident and lacking in confidence, and might even express anxieties about enlarging their own parental role in education, are usually able, with appropriate encouragement and help from the school, to take on such a role; and having done so, go on developing their own knowledge, interest and understanding. Nor does such parental education limit itself to learning to read. A nursery school in London produced small word cards suggesting 'scientific experiments' that parents could undertake with their own children in the home. At the back of the cards, parents were encouraged to write the responses of their children to these, largely Piagetian-based tasks. But the writing was simply a 'prompt' to parents to observe the reactions of their children, and more often, parents simply discussed the outcomes with the nursery teacher.

The cards had two functions: they enabled parents to work with their children at home on a clearly specified task which was enjoyable to both, and which involved language. It was a way, therefore, for parents and children to come together and talk about a common project, the outcome of which was unknown to them. By recording their children's reactions and observations, the cards enabled parents to become more observant of their children's developing minds, and to discuss these observations with other parents as well as the supervisor. In the end, it was a strategy which involved adult education as much as it did child development.

From reporting their own children's observations the parents moved to a demand to learn more about the tests themselves, and from there, to a desire to come to grips with Piagetian development models. The nursery school acted as the innovating agency, the source of support, encouragement and resources.

Such varied approaches stimulate a sense of 'self-worth' in both children and the family, but they can only 'work' if parents feel that they have an equal share in the enterprise; when, in effect, they feel in 'control' of the provision itself.

It is this feeling of 'shared endeavour' which lies at the heart of the British and Dutch playgroup movements, in which parents (mainly mothers), operate their own playgroups in local halls and homes for children aged between two-and-a-half and five years. There are, currently, about 14,000 such playgroups throughout the United Kingdom, run voluntarily by parents themselves, charging families a small amount per session of some two-and-a-half hours a morning. Local authorities often give grants to these playgroups — which exist alongside maintained nursery schools and nursery classes — to defray costs of hiring premises and buying equipment, and at present such playgroups provide the largest source of pre-school experience for children in the United Kingdom.

In the Netherlands, playgroups have grown from only 57 in 1969 to some 2,290 by 1975 (Singer, E., OECD, 1980). Most of the Dutch playgroups are operated by the VVAO (Association of Women with an Academic Education), and have quite specific characteristics. They are usually open for some three hours in the mornings, they mainly cater for children from two to four, and their control is in the hands of local parents. The groups are normally run by a qualified worker, whose function is a mixture of care-giving, nursing and teaching, and is therefore better summarized by the Dutch word *leidster* just as the English prefer to speak about a playgroup leader. Again, like the British version, many Dutch playgroups are subsidized by their municipalities.

Rather like some of the Head Start projects in the United States, many playgroups see their main value not merely to the child, but as a source of involvement for the child's parents. In the 37th Session of the UNESCO International Conference on Education, held in Geneva in 1979, the United States reported that within Head Start programmes, 'parents are able to learn that they are able to control the course of their lives, and learn to work within the community structure to reach their own goals, and in the process develop more positive attitudes towards the community and its institutions, such as schools. Moreover, such participation is also good for the children. As parents gain self-confidence, and inner direction, they pass on these attitudes to their children.'

It is this sense of personal confidence, awareness and involvement in what is intrinsically a self-controlled venture which marks the play-group as a particularly useful form of pre-school experience for the community and the family. In saying this, we must not blind ourselves to the fact that most playgroups in the United Kingdom are sited in urban areas of either 'average' or 'well-to-do' socioeconomic districts (van der Eyken, W. *et al.,* 1982) or that, because they operate for only a limited number of hours — usually in the morning — they are mainly available to families where the mother does not go out to work; or, if she works, does so part-time. Their other difficulty is that, because playgroups are run by parents themselves and staffed by them with often the help of a supervisor trained specifically on playgroup courses, the quality of provision can vary greatly. This variability in quality is, however, partly a product of the way in which educational resources are distributed within United Kingdom local authorities, in which the voluntary sector is largely left to manage on its own resources, without any of the back-up support of advisers, inspectors, medical supervision and other aids which maintained nursery schools and primary schools receive as part of their own supportive, professional network. If such support were to be extended to the voluntary sector, and if as a result resources were spread more evenly between the two, then this particular issue might not be the cause of concern which it is today.

But while the playgroup model may be inappropriate for many member States which seek to provide a more centralized, overall system of pre-schooling, it does provide a number of pointers in parental participation which are valuable for the future. In particular, by being non-institutional non-threatening to many parents who react negatively to the school system, and by offering a vehicle for both community control and self-help, playgroups also act as a form of adult education for the community. That is to say, parents who being with a primary concern for their own children learn, by working with other children, to foster their own interest in child development. This learning is amplified in the playgroup movement by a series of courses for parents, enhanced today by the Open University's courses which are pursued in the family home. By furthering the learning of parents in this way, playgroups build on the natural concern of parents to help their children by providing the opportunity for such parents to develop their own skills and knowledge, rather than seeing this gap in their knowledge as a reason for dismissing parents from an institution staffed by professional workers who, by definition, are expected to know more than the family.

What the playgroup movement also demonstrates is that parental control is not a concept which can be imposed from outside, but is an organic feeling of confidence which grows through participation. Sandgren (OECD/CERI, 1978), describes the experience of a crèche in Bologna where the ideal of parental control was, as it were, imposed from the health authority upon the community it was intended to serve:

> After two meetings, the parents completely lost interest . . . . When the crèche was first opened, not only were its organizational arrangements already finalized, but they were presented to the parents as being extremely efficient, valid, forward-looking (and therefore difficult to improve). On the one hand, therefore, parents were asked to intervene in management, thus encouraging the delegation of responsibility, but on the other hand, they were offered no real area of intervention.

The issue of parental control is also at the heart of the *gestione sociale*, a series of experiments inspired by the political Left in Italy to increase the involvement and control by ordinary citizens of public institutions, and an attempt to create new forms of representative democracy. The major aim of this movement seeks to place the control of both pre- and primary schooling in the hands, not merely of parents, but of the community as a whole, including the trade unions (Mantovani, S., 1978). This wider involvement is intended to remedy the possible control of the facilities by a 'clique' of parents with the necessary talents and motivation for such an undertaking, and has the further advantage that it can lead to action in new directions. One example quoted by Mantovani of the way unions were influential in broadening the outlook of the school was an agreement that, instead of reducing working hours, 20 paid hours per month of the staff-time was agreed should be available for in-service training or for committee meetings and assemblies.

One of the main targets for the *gestione sociale* movement is a State education system which is seen to be increasingly hierarchical in character, with head teachers, staff, assistants, non-teaching staff and, somewhere beyond, parents forming a pyramid of authority against which the prospect of change or adaptation to local conditions has little chance of success. Mantovani underlines this point by reflecting that teachers often react with surprise to the request of working-class parents that, above all, their children should acquire such basic skills as reading and writing, in order not to face failure in the elementary school. Within the pre-school, however, teachers tend to believe that there are different tasks which have priority, such as 'to allow the child to express itself freely', and that the learning of specific skills is inappropriate. This stress on 'freedom of expression' is, however, difficult for children with lower socioeconomic backgrounds, with child-rearing experiences which are either authoritarian or restricted. The outcome may therefore be that such children are asked to conform to an inappropriate model of childhood, leading to frustration and lack of benefit for either parents or child. It is this 'culture clash' which the *gestione sociale* seeks to attack by placing control firmly in the hands of the community. It is worth stressing that in itself, such diversified control is no guarantee that the subsequent provision will meet the real needs of children, or that it will not, in its turn, become an ideological battleground between different groups within the community. Indeed, there are some indications that the problems stemming from such diversified control lead to both confusion and lack of direction and that, in their very zeal to tackle the perceived inequalities, they might saddle the educational system with other, equally intractable, difficulties (Andreolo, R., Council of Europe, 1977).

One imaginative attempt to 'open up the nursery school' to parents is the Children's House, built in an industrial town in Cheshire, in the United Kingdom. Tomlinson (Council of Europe, 1977), in describing this venture, says that:

> We did not envisage it either as a formal nursery school or even a formal playgroup, but rather hoped to provide a situation where mothers could come to make friends and to bring with them their children of pre-school age to try out the facilities and to learn from each other and from the staff available what children enjoy and what they need for maximum growth.

Notably, again, the Children's House was designed to be used by the community itself, on the assumption that mothers and their pre-school children aged from nought to five would be at home to make use of it. On this well-founded assumption, the design broke away from the institutional model of a nursery school by providing an essentially 'domestic' form of provision, with a range of pleasant seats in bright designs, colours and textures, which would recreate the essential features of a family home. The centre itself was sited in an open area, so that it was surrounded by a large outdoor play area and recreation facilities for children of all ages to use either alone, or in the company of their parents.

The Children's House in Cheshire is a concrete example of Doxiades' principle that 'support for families should have as their aim to enable them to perform their allocated function and not to be replaced in performing that function'. It does so, not merely by being as flexible as possible – parents can walk in at any time, and use it in a variety of ways – but it also harnesses the professional resources of the community to provide services in an easy and accessible way for families. The social workers, the health visitor and the teacher 'drop in' or are available for appointments, if and when the parents need them. This underlines that pre-schooling, and indeed the whole educational process, is not simply about schools and teachers, but about a variety of services, all of which have major contributions to make to the health and welfare of the family and the community. If we want to help these particularly disadvantaged families, we must ensure that all such services reach them in ways which make it possible for them to benefit from such help. As the European Ministers responsible for Family Affairs, in the final communiqué following their meeting in Athens in May 1979, observed:

> The principle of equality of opportunity has so far been discussed almost exclusively in connection with education. However, it has been found that school cannot, on its own, adequately fulfil this function .... The child's future thus depends largely on the family background and environment, and it is therefore mainly by helping family situations that children can be helped.

It is an attempt to work with this family background and environment which prompts a remarkable experiment in both pre-school and community education on the island of Sicily, at Ispica (Scheffknecht, J.J., Council of Europe, 1978). This project takes as its clients not merely the young children, but the whole family, using normal nursery school facilities in the town, but at the same time basing its adult education programme on the parental problems facing the family. It is out of concern expressed by the parents for information about child development, nutrition, children's illnesses that an adult education programme has been constructed, which is focussed largely on their role as parents, but which at the same time has as its immediate concern the parents' children themselves.

Families, including their children, share activities between both pre-school and adult education. They tackle similar topics, they take part in the same community activities, make the same trips together, share entertainment. As a result of their first, immediate preoccupations, the parents move on to study problems affecting their community, but which still impinge on the welfare of their children: the provision of play areas in their town; the problems of controlling dangerous traffic; the educational value of shared holidays. From there, the adults begin to tackle other, related issues, such as the care of the aged, the planning of their town, local legislation and related topics.

This form of 'community education and involvement' is obviously most suited to a community where educational standards may be low, but it would be quite wrong to conclude that it is only applicable to 'marginal' economies. For a very similar project, also attempting to work with both the pre-school, primary school and indeed secondary school, as well as with the adult population, has been conducted for four years in the very heart of Glasgow, in Scotland. A small team of teachers and community workers moved into the small community of Moorpark, in Govan, a part of the city which was being re-developed but which suffered from considerable 'urban blight' and social deprivation. The aim was not simply to provide an element of pre-schooling for the young children, but to work with the whole community of Moorpark to see themselves as the prime educators of their children, within their own family circumstances. In order to enable the families to be supported in their efforts, however, the team also worked with the professional resources in the area — the teachers, playgroup staff and health visitors.

There is an international problem of inner-city educational mismatch. One symptom is academic under-achievement.

Among the children of Moorpark, their ability is noticeably higher than their attainment.

This problem is specific, but it is not isolated. Therefore, it cannot be solved by the educational institutions alone. It is part of a complex web of problems concerned with politics, employment, housing, social norms and public opinion. Any solution must take these complex factors into account. The Govan project is an attempt to deal with a specific educational problem within the total reality of a small, fairly typical housing estate in Glasgow (Strathclyde Experiment in Education: Govan Project – Interim Report, 1977.)

One tool which the project used extensively throughout was the teaching of language skills. It set up a community library, and encouraged parents to bring their children to it and to choose books together, with the purpose of stimulating parents to read to their children at home. It organized adult literacy classes. It arranged 'story-telling' sessions for parents and children. It operated on the local issue of control of the tenants' hall. It tried to tackle the issue of local youth unemployment. And it organized a number of local events, in which the community itself planned and ran projects of their own. There was a family workshop, in which parents came together to make masks, kites, puppets and finally, a huge paper dragon. These were later brought together to form the centre of a street play. Fourteen families were involved in a pantomime workshop. And there was a reading workshop, where parents and their children came together, hearing stories and discussing the ideas behind the teaching of reading.

The workers went into the homes of the Moorpark families, in a sense seeking to act as 'change-agents' to stimulate the educative process within the home itself, to raise the status of educational processes in families where 'schooling' was associated, traditionally, with 'failure', and where relations between home and school were, if not totally negative, at best operated on a level of mutual suspicion.

The Govan concept of 'total education for the whole community', like the Ispica project, reflect a recognition that, for many disadvantaged communities, relations between professional services such as education and the population it seeks to serve have to overcome a long legacy of failure and despair. But they also demonstrate the opportunities that exist, within communites that do not suffer from such ravages of dereliction, to build a more creative relationship between what education has to offer and what communities need. They indicate that the education of young children is not simply a matter of 'schooling' the children or 'dealing with' their parents, but can become a truly creative partnership in a joint enterprise that affects everyone.

For many societies, such 'total' involvement is neither practical nor desirable, and we must not be seduced by novelty any more than we can be complacent about tradition. The evidence available indicates that children will thrive in their education if their own families demonstrate a positive and purposeful recognition of its value, and if the child within the family feels himself to be a person with self-esteem living within that family.

But if the family is depressed, either by socioeconomic forces exerting pressures upon it from the outside, or by psychological pressures from within — and all the indicators suggest that more and more families are affected in this way — then confidence in the purposes of education and its relevance to the problems of the family will decline, and be replaced by indifference, or a sense of alienation, which is transmitted to the child. It does not automatically follow that the child will demonstrate learning difficulties, or itself become depressed, for children are not mere barometers of their family's health, but individuals in their own right, having their own power of adaptation and initiative.

For many children, however, an imbalance between the climate of the home and the school will indeed result in detrimental results, and no amount of 'information sharing' between home and school will bridge the chasm. What we must ensure is that schools become more flexible to parental needs and concerns, that they are open to new ways of responding to parental wishes and anxieties, that they strive ceaselessly to ensure that all services, and not simply those formally described as 'educational' are brought to bear on the needs of the family. In addition, schools must explore how they can bring their resources to bear on the needs of the entire family, and not merely one isolated member of it, so as to stimulate a 'process of learning' within the family itself.

That is the task of working 'with, and through' the family.

CHAPTER SIX

The Enabling Environment

In many European countries, the most obvious and necessary need is to provide a more appropriate level of educational provision for young children, and to encourage this provision to work more directly both with families and the community. But of equal importance, the State has a self-interest in ensuring that central policies are so designed as to enhance the ability of families to function to the greatest possible benefit of children. Just as families seek to provide the conditions for the development of independence of their own children, and recognize that overly-dependent children represent a lack of growth, so the State has a role in enabling families to function; to provide the enabling environment for them to do so. But how? What is it that hampers European families in their chosen task of raising their children?

From a recent survey of some 9,000 families within the nine countries of the EEC (Commission of the European Communities, 1979), it is clear that the greatest difficulties lie not in the field of education itself, but are concerned with the resources available to families, particularly of finance and housing. The survey dealt with three groups of families: those who did not have children, those who were currently supporting children up to the age of fifteen, and those whose children had grown up. Table 6.1 deals only with the replies of families *who were actually bringing up children*, though the ages of the children themselves were between one and 15, and therefore do not necessarily reflect the problems of those with very young children. Nevertheless, the results are clearcut, and show not only that finance and housing are the two issues which are by far the most important for families, but also that there are important differences between countries in the problems facing families.

In the smaller EEC countries (Belgium, Luxembourg, Netherlands),

Table 6.1: *Main problems encountered by parents with children aged under 15 years of age*

Problems (A maximum of three)*	EEC %	Bel. %	Fed. Rep. Ger. %	Den. %	Fr. %	Ire. %	Ital. %	Lux. %	Neth. %	UK %
Money	27	7	9	29	29	42	32	12	8	29
Housing	25	10	18	31	27	20	32	8	13	18
Having to leave children with someone else	16	9	18	12	18	3	27	7	3	13
Lack of parks, etc.	16	6	9	13	19	16	18	16	15	18
Lack of sports and leisure facilities	15	7	7	9	17	15	19	8	5	20
Working hours and school hours do not coincide	12	3	9	20	10	6	10	8	4	11
School holidays	11	5	11	15	14	5	9	6	4	10
Getting children to school	10	3	8	13	10	15	11	9	5	7
Living in problem area	6	3	2	4	7	3	10	2	6	5
Other problems	2	3	6	1	3	2	1	4	3	3
No problems mentioned	32	69	46	35	29	31	20	58	58	30

*Totals add up to more than 100 per cent because respondents could name more than one problem.

Source: Commission of the European Communities, 1979, *Europeans and their Children*, Table VII, p. 28.

families would appear to have less major problems than in the larger ones, such as France, the United Kingdom, Italy and, to a lesser extent, West Germany. If we take only these four, we find that their difficulties are, again, somewhat different. In France, money and housing are the major problems. In the Federal Republic, it is housing, as well as the severe difficulties caused by the restriction of school hours, which means that parents have to find others with whom to leave their children during the afternoon. In the United Kingdom, money is the largest single problem, and in Italy, it is both shortage of money and housing.

Even though the data relate to families raising children of a widely differing age range, what is clear is that educational benefits can only be reaped on the back of social policies that provide adequate resources of finance, housing and good health and that, without these prerequisites, education by itself can only offer a limited service. This is notably true for larger families, who in the EEC survey were shown to have more problems and with greater frequency. It is in this context that the provision of child benefit allowances becomes crucial. One in six of those in receipt of such allowances said that these benefits were 'vital'; more than half felt they were either 'vital' or 'very useful', regardless of the actual size of the allowances themselves.

The survey data offer encouragement for those countries, notably Belgium, West Germany, the Netherlands and France, which step up their benefit payments for families with more than two children, so that in effect the larger families get more. Such additional payments do not, of themselves, prompt people to have more children, for as we have already seen (in Chapter Two), there exists throughout Europe a strong and continuing movement towards smaller families. But they do ensure that as costs rise, those with the heaviest burdens and responsibilities are given additional support.

Moreover, the survey suggests (as common sense would dictate), that the most powerful elements of a State family policy lie in the realms of economic and housing policies. Under these broad headings there fall, of course, many different aspects of both economic and social policy that vitally affect every family; not only the fight against inflation, issues of employment and of social security, of levels of both direct and indirect taxation, but of housing rebates, and of charges made for services like education and health. These demonstrate that while communities continue to reflect great inequalities in these basic areas of provision, pursuit of the 'Just Society' through the sole medium of education is largely a myth. As Sandgren (1980), has put it recently:

Despite all expectations which have been put forward for the potential of education as an instrument of equality, and despite a considerable re-direction of resources within the educational sector, all experience points to the impossibility of solving basic equality problems within the framework of education. To give everyone the same prerequisites for personal development and participation in the development of society is outside the realm of education.

What this means is that the wider objectives of educational policy have their roots in policies other than education, and that the life that three-to-eight year olds lead in Europe in the Eighties will very largely be decided by factors outside the field either of the family or the school.

Consider, for example, the way that different European countries actually support families. The pattern and level of benefits and services for children within the nine EEC countries has recently been the subject of a detailed study by Bradshaw and Piachaud (1980). Their figures (for January 1980), were as up-to-date as possible, and their study went well beyond a comparison of family allowances and social benefits to consider all kinds of State support, and the effect these had on four different types of families. Table 6.2 shows the relative value of existing family allowances for a two-child family on average earnings. The differences must be seen in the context of overall child support. Even so, they are revealing, for they show that Ireland's family allowance is currently worth only about 13 per cent of the Belgian family allowance. Belgian allowances, indeed, are the most generous in the EEC both in absolute and relative terms, with the smallest allowances paid by Ireland and Italy. Moreover, while it is now common throughout the EEC for family allowances to be tax-free, not all of them were index-linked, and the study showed that index-linked allowances tended to be the most generous (measured at a time of rising inflation).

Again, there were important differences about the details of how payments are made, and to whom. In Britain, family allowances are paid in mid-week. But in the Netherlands and Denmark they were paid quarterly, in West Germany every two months and in every other country, monthly. This means that the family allowance itself could be used for larger items of expenditure, rather than having to be saved up by the family itself. It involved a form of compulsory saving.

Table 6.2: Value of family allowances for a two-child family on average earnings January, 1980

	Family allowance as percentage of gross average earnings	Equivalent purchasing power £
Belgium	14.1	842
Denmark	3.9	266
West Germany	6.0	400
France	8.4	402
Ireland	2.2	113
Italy	3.1	155
Luxembourg	7.0	567
Netherlands	9.1	589
United Kingdom	8.7	416

Source: Corden, A., Piachaud, D., and Bradshaw, J., 'How Europe
meets family costs', New Society, October 23, 1980,
pp. 159–161.

Although basic education is provided free in all EEC countries, there is considerable variation in the fringe benefits associated with it. Only Britain and Denmark provided books and stationery free, and only Britain offered a free, fully-subsized mid-day meal to families who could not afford to pay for it; a benefit of considerable value to the individual child, and potentially of direct relevance to educational attainment.

Family allowances serve no good purpose if other charges that families incur in supporting their children simply erode them. In all countries in the EEC except West Germany and Britain, for example, a proportion of primary health care costs had to be met by the family, and in some countries, like Ireland and the Netherlands, this could have a considerable impact on family incomes. While all EEC countries except Belgium and Luxembourg had some kind of direct subsidy scheme for local authority housing, for example, under which rents vary with income, the ways these operated in the different countries differed considerably, and reflected very different policies. Britain had the most generous allowance scheme for families at the lower income levels, but France helped those on average earnings and gave the highest subsidy to families with children. It also had the most progressive policy, of helping large families more than small ones.

When all these forms of family support were put together, as the researchers managed to do, several important features emerged for State family policy. The variations between countries were considerable, from Belgium and France, with strong family policies generously weighted towards larger families, to Denmark and Britain, in the middle, weighted towards lower income and smaller families, to Italy and Ireland, with relatively ungenerous support. But such a comparison also showed that, of all the types of family support examined, *family allowances* made the largest contribution and that here, Belgium, France, the Netherlands and Luxembourg were a long way ahead in giving such direct financial assistance to families.

To those States which would argue that economic support for families must await an upturn in their own national economies, or follow in the development of a larger economic 'cake', there is one final lesson from this research. It is that there was no direct connection between the level of an economy and the degree of child support. *It is simply not true that the richest countries in the EEC also have the most generous family support schemes.* For child support is the outcome of social, rather than economic, policies.

If we now look back, beyond these basic issues, to the survey of European families, we see, from Table 6.1, that there are also other factors that affect family care for children. One in six families, for instance, felt that having to leave children with someone else constitutes a problem for them. They complained, too, of the lack of adequate open spaces where children can play in safety, about the shortage of sports and recreational facilities (this would most affect older children), and having to make arrangements for children to be looked after during school holidays. Partly, these problems are environmental and administrative, but underlying many of them is the unspoken – and often unmentioned – clash between the demands of the modern industrial-commercial world, and the call on family time and resources that children inevitably make.

It is worth repeating, because it is so essential to the whole issue of education in Europe, that in many European cities and neighbourhoods, the classic 'two-parent Parsonian family' (after Talcott Parsons, the American sociologist who described the nature of this type of family), forms perhaps only one quarter of the households within the community (see, for example, the UK Study Commission on the Family, 1980, Table 1, p. 17). One-parent families, or families composed of stepmothers and stepfathers, or of parents who are not legally married, or of children who have been fostered and adopted, now comprise sizeable proportions of child-rearing households. Thus while many countries have moved at least some way along the road to providing more equitable arrangements for women to enter the labour market (arrangements which are often negated by a lack of adequate day-care), the more fundamental problem of providing a wide variety of families with the resources to shoulder their parenting responsibilities has yet to be tackled. What those EEC parents did *not* say – because they were not asked – is that the most important resource, apart from money and housing, is time. Time to be with a child when it is ill, time to be home when a child returns from school, time to take a child to school, . . . *being a parent takes time.* Yet on arrangements to provide maternal and paternal leave, to shorten working hours for parents with young children, to enable parents to have flexitime work-patterns, without penalizing them financially – on these aspects, there is still much to be done.

So central governments have both a facilitating task to perform, and an educative role to pursue. This is not a programme that can be under-taken overnight, but it can declare its intentions; as some countries, such as Sweden, have already done. It can indicate the direction in which it wishes to travel, and in doing so, create a climate for discussion and debate about ways of reaching its goal. It can stimulate, with-out raising unrealistic expectations, a social awareness of the needs of families and their children. It can even encourage experimentation.

In doing so, however, member States must recognize that, even within their own administration of services for young children, there are often serious problems of overlap, duplication and simple confusion between conflicting agencies. The difficulty is basically between the concept of 'care' and 'education'. In general, 'care', with a socio-medical bias, is provided for children from infancy to three years or even beyond, to school age. 'Education', on the other hand, is aimed at the post-toddler stage, from about three years of age. In some countries, these two functions are administered by different agencies, delivering different services in separate institutions manned by staffs with different training, remuneration and objectives.

In Norway, for instance, the relevant department for the control of kindergartens is, deliberately, called the Family Affairs and Equal Status Department. As the Ministry of Social Welfare, whose Depart-ment it is, has itself said of this arrangement: 'The provision and operation of kindergartens is a very important part of family policy, and must be viewed in connection with other measures for the benefit of families with young children.' Indeed, the most recent legislation on kindergarten provision in Norway arose originally out of the so-called White Book, or *Stortingsmelding*, on the living conditions of families, which also dealt with issues such as shorter working hours for parents and the right to leave for parents whose children were ill.

What Norway has recognized by this administrative division is that all educational administration not only incorporates elements of 'care' within it, but also has important social consequences. When, for example, British nursery schools and classes operate from nine in the morning until half-past-three in the afternoon, it is on the assumption that parents (i.e. mothers) are free to take and fetch them at these times. When schools do not provide a mid-day meal, it is on the assumption that the child will be fed elsewhere. When the German system offers only morning sessions, it is again on the understanding that parents – or someone else – are available to look after these children for the rest of the day. These are social assumptions, which hold less and less true in our changing society. But in the sense that they are more true for some groups than for others, they are also assumptions which carry strong class overtones.

So, in a different sense, are the divisions between 'care' and 'education', for they have created a hierarchy of power and resources, in which the younger, less skilled and most poorly paid are locked into the 'caring' function, while status, training resources, higher salaries and career structures are reserved for the educational sector. As Tizard (1980) commented: 'In all countries, teachers get far more pay, work far shorter hours and have far longer holidays than child care staff.'

The outcome means that, with limited career prospects and poor pay, care provision is almost exclusively staffed by young women whose chances of crossing over to the educational sector are blocked by different entry qualifications and incomatible training requirements. What suffers is the caring function.

One popular way out of this confusion is to encourage 'coordination' of services; to seek to bring together, sometimes under one roof, the provision of the very young in care and those using pre-school services. In England, a series of such 'combined centres', as they are called, has recently been created and a study conducted as to their effectiveness. The results are not greatly encouraging.

The categorization of children according to specific needs, the differences in training, experience and working conditions of staff in nurseries and the lack of clear consensus regarding aims and practice are all issues which must be tackled if any attempt to eradicate the artificial distinction between day care and education is to succeed (Ferri, E., 1980).

This echoes the words of warning given by Weiss *et al.* (1980) about such experiments in the United States, and the observation that, far from achieving some form of symbiosis of mutual dependency and supportiveness, the different perspectives and interests of the groups thus brought together often results in a depressing lack of genuine cooperation. As one practitioner once remarked: 'The only thing we shared was the Kleenex box!'

Attempts to coordinate irreconcilable interests and groups fail precisely because such efforts are an admission that the two sectors cannot reasonably be combined: why, otherwise, not combine them in the first instance? Sometimes the urge for coordination comes from a deep desire for greater order and rationality. 'The staggering number of agencies, the multiple sources of funding, the elaborate division of labour among agencies and among professions, the overlapping lines of authority deriving from local, regional and national administration of policy for children' – these, as Weiss has put it, almost cry out for some comprehensive reform. But instead of reform, the administrative solution too often lies in placing all the elements in a container, shaking vigorously, and hoping that the result will produce a palatable cocktail when, almost invariably, the outcome is, rather, an unappetising pot pourri.

The real need, given the fairly recent development, in most European countries, of elaborated systems of pre-school education, is to now set about to reform the entire field of early childhood support and education; to develop as Kurt Lüscher has suggested (OECD, 1980), policies which will:

a) enable children to grow up within their own families;
b) attempt to influence the family environment;
c) complement the family to provide child activity outside the home;
d) supplement the family in times of need or crisis.

It is in the latter two areas of 'complementing' and 'supplementing' the family that the need arises for a reorganized, comprehensive and adequately trained work-force which will be both commited to children and dedicated to working with them 'through the family'. One stratagem would be to do away with the current divisions between c) and d); to recognize that 'care' and 'education' are part of a single, seamless raiment, and to thereby make a single government department responsible for the entire field. An alternative stratagem would be to clearly limit the two fields, such as offering 'care' to those under three years of age, with 'education' encompassing the older children's provision. Every possible permutation will pose problems of administration, demarcation, funding, resources and status and clearly there will be no universal solution. Nor should a desire for clarity and neatness impinge on the real need for flexibility and local variation. In the end, we are concerned with the needs of children and their parents, and any solution which made that goal more distant would be retrograde.

That the reorganization of the present provision is necessary is, however, hardly in doubt. What it underlines is that we are beginning to see the need to move away from traditional patterns of staff towards the evolution of three different types of professional workers in the education and care of young children.

First is the teacher of early childhood education, spanning the three-to-eight age range or even possibly the three-to-11/13 age range, but specializing, perhaps in a narrower age band. In this model, teachers would receive a common training, together with specialized tuition, in primary nursery education. Secondly, there is a new type of community worker, the early childhood resource coordinator, drawn from a variety of sources – education, health, social work or the voluntary sector – whose basic aim is to coordinate local resources and to work with a variety of provision and needs. A pioneering course to produce such 'coordinators' has recently been launched at the Roehampton Institute for Higher Education, London (Condry, G., 1980).

But perhaps the most crucial need is for a reappraisal of the role of child-care staff who man the provision which offers either 'care' or 'education' institutions at the pre-school level. As Tizard (1980) has pointed out:

> If there is to be participation by volunteers, parents and para-professionals in the nursery service, new relations between

professionals and other adults must be fostered. The role of the fully-trained professional will then be, to a much greater extent than in the past, one of working with adults rather than children; professional training must equip them for this.

One important feature of training as at present constituted is that it provides a passport to both power and status; that it creates a gulf between the trained and the untrained. But we have already postulated that there is a great need for a greater rapport between families, who bring to child-care and education a localized folk-wisdom, and those who are formally employed to offer care. One barrier to this rapport is the entry qualifications for membership of the professional qualification, and in some countries with a particularly strong voluntary sector, this division will be reflected in terms of those with considerable practice and experience against those with an academic, but largely theoretic background. We need to produce a system in which the parent, the volunteer, the mother or father with every experience and wisdom, can find a place within the system. As Singer (1980) has proposed, we need a training system in which formal qualifications alone are not paramount, in which courses include a part-time or evening element so that those among the general population are not excluded, and in which the value of practical experience, such as running a playgroup or raising one's own family, is recognized.

Moreover, these people — who have so much to offer but are so often excluded for petty, administrative reasons from the very fields in which they are most competent — require a clearly-defined career structure in which further experience and study will be compensated and rewarded. As Tizard has commented (1980):

> Pre-school services need to draw more widely, for their paid workers, on two groups in the community with much more potentiality to offer: young men, and middle-aged and older people of both sexes, especially those with experience of raising their own families. Apart from the reserves of talent and experience in these two groups, largely untapped at present, the current female monopoly of staffing, especially with so many younger women employed, reinforces the limited range of adult relationships that young children are increasingly faced with. To encourage the recruitment of middle-aged men and women, but also because it is not clear that existing training is necessarily the

best we could have, more emphasis should be put on in-service training and less on longer, general courses.

What we are arguing for is a more integrated structure of professional training which moves at the initial stage to an involvement of parents, young adults and voluntary workers within the 'care' field, but which leaves open the possibility of those with initiative and talent to move into the more specialized fields of education, health or social work, through the medium of experience and in-service training. Just as we argued earlier that the barrier between pre-school teaching staff and primary teaching staff created barriers of salary, or expertise, of mobility and of career structure, so within the echelons of day-care staff current practice creates difficulties which in fact result in an artificial segregation which countermands the lessons of child psychology and psychiatry.

Children need adults. From the child's point of view, the background and training that those adults have received is incidental to the value their presence makes within either a day-care centre or a pre-school institution. If we move perceptively towards a more community-oriented approach to pre-school care and education, it is imperative that we provide opportunities for adults themselves to move into this field, and to progress through it. The British Pre-School Playgroups movement has seen this fundamental point by making available to parents with an interest in young children (see Wolfson, J., OECD, 1980), a series of graduated courses which, beginning with the most fundamental, gradually increases the theoretical content for those who seek to become supervisors of playgroups or even advisors of others. What is missing, at present, is some transitional procedure whereby those who have gained such experiences within the voluntary sector might, through their experience and practice, be able to apply their skills and knowledge in the more professionalized areas of practice.

There is, at present, no consensus among member States about the nature of training or of the qualifications for staff involved in early childhood education (Corbett, OECD, 1980). Some place an almost traditional weight on theoretical work; others give some credence to practical experience. There are, moreover, a plethora of other specialists involved in the field. Psychologists, counsellors, school doctors, nurses, vocational counsellors and social workers are all involved in the three-to-eight age range: speech therapists, physical therapists and teachers all have their roles to play.

It follows that the pre-school teacher will, increasingly, want to change her role from that of a narrow specialist to an 'enabler', working within a team, bringing resources to the children and families and stimulating local involvement and initiatives. With resources such as nursery schools and primary schools becoming increasingly expensive, there is an economic necessity to use such facilities to their utmost. Pre-school teachers, working closely with the local community, may well be in a position to suggest, at the local level, how this might best be done, how educational resources might be adapted to meet the changing needs of a community.

But such a creative, innovative role will not be possible while member States retain the present divisions between the teaching staff of pre-schooling and primary education. To maintain such segregation is to permanently stultify the pre-school sector of the education system. That is a message which has been well taken by the Netherlands, as it pursues its ambitious target to integrate pre-school and primary education into a new, integrated *basisonderwijs*, covering the entire age range from four to 12 years. Since 1977, some 4,500 pairs of nursery schools and primary schools have been involved in a research project to identify difficulties, but by 1983, when the new system comes into general practice, virtually all of the country's pre- and primary schools will have been linked into the new format. Hand-in-hand with this programme the Dutch authorities have pursued an examination of new in-service training courses and refresher courses (Ministry of Education, Netherlands, 1980, p. 34), and have recognized the fact that the 'new' primary school teacher's brief will 'have to stretch beyond the boundaries of the classroom or the school building' (Innovatie Commissie OB, 1980). In its advice on new forms of preparation, the Commission in charge of this development has stressed that the training of teachers would need to take into account an understanding of the involvement of the community, and of the diverse welfare organizations and resources which schools should harness to enable them to perform their task.

Unlike in the Netherlands, the Belgian reforms to integrate pre-school and primary education do not include the creation of a single teaching force and other countries, too, while examining changes in their pre-school teacher training, still adhere to a two-tier system of teacher status. In Austria, according to Corbett (1980), nursery school teachers enjoy a lower status than primary school teachers. Those undertaking a kindergarten or nursery school course can begin at the age of 14, without completing their full secondary education, whereas those wishing to qualify for primary teaching must first finish 13 years of general education, followed by two years of higher education. And in Sweden, which has pursued some important reforms in the programmes of training pre-school teachers (Askling, 1979), there also remains a division between pre-school and primary school staffs.

To begin to dismantle these professional barriers, though a formidable task, will not be enough to produce a more outward-looking, community-involved, innovative teacher task force. As the Rapporteur to the Council for Cultural Cooperation's Symposium on the 'Training of teaching staff engaged in pre-school education' in Leyden in 1973 remarked:

> Whatever the system, teacher training is not a secondary problem to be solved after the institutions have been established and put into operation. We all agree that the question of teacher training is the keystone of the whole system. To think about teacher training is to think about the whole of the educational system; to wish to change, transform or, as some will say, revolutionize teacher training necessarily implies to change, transform or revolutionize the education system.

What that Symposium also stressed was the need to see the education of pre-school staffs as a process of continuing education. 'The training of the educational staff for the pre-school level should be permanent training, i.e. an initial basic training to be followed up by continued training throughout a career.'

There are a number of important reasons why the training of teachers working in the pre-school sector should be reformed. The first is that the whole field of child development is one which is expanding at a very fast rate, and the last decade has seen an explosion of knowledge and information about early childhood education and care. So simply to remain aware of new developments will require updating procedures to be introduced. There are, in addition, new ways of working, and even regarding, pre-school resources, particularly in its relations to communities and families, but also as the vehicle for the delivery of their services such as social work and health care. But in addition, there is now a general recognition that in working 'with, and through, the family', as the Council of Europe Conference Declaration put it, pre-schooling — and, indeed, primary education as well — is seen as merely one component of a much wider focus of attention which seeks to educate the entire family.

In this sense, pre-schooling is a facet of adult education. It is this conception of early childhood education which lies at the heart of the Italian *gestione sociale* reforms, the English and Dutch pre-school playgroups movement, some of the Danish experiments in communal daycare and many other, enlightened experiments and projects throughout Europe. The concept of dealing with the entire 'ecology of childhood', of supporting and developing the whole environment in which a child grows up, of offering a wide variety of resources to the family; this is a concept which requires a different type of staff.

The essence of this transformation lies in its flexibility, in its ability to respond to local needs and initiatives. There is no single answer to the patterns which might result, other than to state categorically that a single answer is *not* the goal. In the end, the judgement about whether the provision that countries make for the child from three to eight in the educational sector will lie with the people it is meant to serve: does it meet their needs? Does it respond to changes in their environment? Is it flexible enough to cope with such changes? And does it, as a result of providing local support, encourage all children to thrive? If not, do families have an opportunity to alter it, to make it more adaptable? Do families feel that it is part of their social equipment, something which they can regard both as valuable in itself and as something in which they wish to be personally involved? These are the questions that will act as the litmus paper for future provision, and on the answers will depend their future.

Summary

Although this report is limited to a discussion of the education of three-to-eight year olds, the title should not imply that education either does not, or should not, take place before the age of three. Rather, it is a recognition that the discussion is directed, in the first place, to the 23 member States signatory to the Cultural Convention, in most of whose countries it is not until the age of three or later that 'education' is normally provided outside the family home.

This report, therefore, deals largely with the public provision of educational facilities, rather than with the process of education itself; it deals, that is to say, with the problems of 'schooling' rather than with the processes of 'education'. For that reason, and because it is in the first place directed to the Ministers of Education, there is little or no mention of the provisions for day-care made by member States, nor of the often considerable resources devoted within those States to the care of the very young.

At the same time, it sets out to illustrate the relationship between 'education' and 'schooling'; between the private activity of learning and the public activity of teaching; between the individual development of the child and the public provision of resources and facilities for enhancing such development throughout the public sector.

In doing so, the personal views expressed in this paper take a particular stance about the learning process itself, and about the institutions which seek to foster that process. It postulates an 'ecological' view which, simply stated, proposes that every child — and, in particular, every young child — is strongly influenced by its family, its neighbourbood, its environment and its culture, and that it brings to 'schooling' an amalgam of all these influences, together with its own unique personality and characteristics.

In **Chapter One**, the paper seeks to provide a glimpse of the very different ecological backgrounds which the children of Europe bring to their learning, by focussing on the experiences within three member States — Belgium, Denmark and Portugal — of the young child and the educational provision. These three studies were not chosen as in any way representative of Europe as a whole, but rather to demonstrate the great diversity both of traditions and of provision within the 23 States concerned. They were selected as in some way spanning the very wide range of experiences that might be open to European children in the Eighties in countries with different types of system.

These three glimpses of provision within member States nevertheless give rise to a series of important, communal issues, many of which have their focus on the changing pattern of family life. This is the subject of **Chapter Two**, where some of the variables affecting family structure are examined — the shrinking family, the changing family, the more mobile and unstable family — against a common denominator or increasing economic retrenchment. What is postulated in this chapter is that smaller European families, enjoying longer longevity and greater uncertainty of relationships, paradoxically will make greater demands on centralized educational systems, which will find it increasingly difficult to match expectations with resources.

In a nutshell, individual families will increasingly be looking for private quality against public quantity; for personal fulfilment against generalized provision. Moreover, these 'clients' will increasingly have changing needs of their own; they will demand of services that they become more flexible and responsive to local demand. It is argued that these changes create a friction between centralized control and increasingly localized demands, and that the only solution to such friction is to move towards a decentralized model of control, with wider familial involvement in shaping largely localized services.

Chapter Three considers the position of the child in the changing world of Europe in the Eighties. It argues that if education services are to be truly effective, they must consider, not so much the cognitive aspects of education, as the actual role and function of children within society; that 'learning' is closely related to 'relevance'; that health and well-being are essential prerequisites to learning and that self-esteem and a sense of place within the community, may be the key ingredients to a self-motivated child and his family.

Yet even where these issues are successfully reconciled, there remain difficult problems within the education systems themselves and, within this age group, the particular problem of transition from the free-ranging child to motivated scholar – the so-called issue of 'vertical continuity'. How can the transformation be successfully accomplished? In **Chapter Four**, it is argued that some of the most important factors bearing on this question are concerned with the relationships that exist between primary and pre-school provision; between the differing status of teachers, the wide differences in the allocation of resources, but perhaps most importantly, between the differing philosophies that dominate the two sectors, and in particular, how these differences affect the relationships of the two sectors with families.

How can the 'ecology of childhood' – the family and the community – be brought to make a more direct contribution to the educational process, and how can the wider community be given a sense of control over the development of its own childhood? In **Chapter Five**, a number of examples are offered of community-based initiatives in a variety of countries, and the suggestion is made that perhaps a greater diversity of localized approaches to formal schooling, with greater parental involvement and control and decision-making, point the way to future developments.

But how can local involvement be stimulated, when central policies often mitigate against the family? In **Chapter Six**, national family policies are shown to vary widely within Europe, and it is argued that if education ministers wish to promote the 'ecology of childhood' and to maximize their efforts in the educational field, they will have to pay more regard to areas that lie outside their immediate control – housing, family benefits, social administration – which have a direct and important effect on family resources. Moreover, it is argued that within the educational sector, teacher training will have to be reformed not only to bring the pre-school and primary sectors more into harmony, but to regard the teacher of the three-to-eight year olds as primarily a resource within a multidisciplinary service, involving health and social services as well as education.

Such a task, it is suggested, involves not only the education of young children, but rather of entire families, and therefore encompasses a major shift of emphasis towards a greater concern for adult, and continuing, education; for *education permanente*. This in turn means that pre-schooling and primary education will in the future embrace a much wider range of resources within the community, seeing its task in a much broader light, as serving not only the child itself, but the entire 'ecology of childhood'; the changing world of adults within which the child is growing up, and of which it will shortly become a full member.

Part II

Statements Made by Representatives of the Participating States at the Conference

The following extracts, drawn from statements made by representatives of the States participating in the Twelfth Session of the Standing Conference of European Ministers of Education in Lisbon in June 1981, have been edited by Willem van der Eyken. The purpose in editing has been to highlight current issues affecting the education of young children in the 23 States participating in the Conference, or to draw attention to new developments in this field within these States. Deletions have been denoted by the symbol[...].

It is to be noted that the Council of Europe carries no responsibility for either the content or the editing of this section.

Introduction

One of the less heralded aspects of modern European educational reform is that, in different guises, children are being encouraged to begin their formal schooling earlier than ever before. And the trend is downwards. Not only is this the case in those countries, like the Netherlands and Belgium, where the actual age of formal entry into school is actively being lowered, but it is also the *de facto* situation in many other countries, where youngsters are coming into a quasi-state educational system as pre-schoolers. Ireland is perhaps a good example. Although formal education does not begin there until six, it is a fact that most young children in that country are actually at school from the age of four.

We can discern this trait from the statements made by official government spokesmen at the 1981 Standing Conference of Ministers of Education, and begin to perceive at least two key strands that have brought it about. For many Western countries — notably France, West Germany, Belgium and the Netherlands — there is a continuing electoral pressure for more extensive provision at the pre-school level, for ever younger children. There exists now a genuine demand in these countries for pre-school provision for toddlers of the age of two. At the same time, there is a growing concern about what is perceived to be a schism between a burgeoning pre-school sector and the rest of the education system. Moreover, there is evidence, as we have seen in Part 1, that pre-school provision by itself does not rule out subsequent school 'failure' (although it may dampen down the worst effects).

In order to cope with both these concerns, governments are accelerating their efforts to integrate the two sections. The prime examples of such integration are, of course, Belgium and the Netherlands, where the entire pre-school area is being welded together with the primary school into a new form of basic education. But other attempts at a closer integration are also perceptible in the statements that follow. The outcome is that, on the Continent today, a number of education systems are developing schools which, to all intents and purposes, absorb the child from the age of around two years old, and hold it until late adolescence; often, indeed, only to proceed still further into a lengthened period of higher education.

In the course of the debate that Ministers conducted on this issue, it is possible to hear, faintly, that such movements are not being pursued without question. The French, proud of the fact that they now possess enough provision for all children aged three and over, nevertheless worry about the fact that in some *écoles maternelles* one can find 25 two year olds in the charge of a single teacher, and the Irish, conscious of the reality that 'pre-school education is a fact of educational life' nevertheless feel concerned to express some scepticism about the processes involved. But it was left to the representative of the Holy See — speaking from the privileged position of lacking an electorate of young families — to observe that elaborate systems of education, involving an ever more zealous bureaucracy, were not what was required. For the Holy See, as some other observers, cannot fail to notice the inevitable logic of such burgeoning systems. As more and more children, of a younger age, move into the pre-schools of Europe, the pressure to make such attendance compulsory, and hence enforce a certain uniformity of attendance, becomes almost irresistible. The movement towards a lowering of formal educational entry is merely a recognition of this tendency.

One of the most worrying aspects, for European states, about such a trend is its cost, and it is no slip of the tongue that some delegates referred to families in terms of 'responsibilities', as well as their need to be involved in the process of pre-schooling. Costs are undoubtedly a major factor, and an escalating one, on national budgets which strive to cope with high levels of unemployment and a continuing financial recession. Moreover, these costs are increased when states, like Luxembourg, attempt to cope with large proportions of immigrant labour and seek to cater for what is, increasingly, a multi-cultural community.

The extent to which electorates now demand such increased facilities for their young children is often prompted by financial considerations. Life in many European countries is today so expensive that no single bread-winner can hope to support a family. So against the costs of increased pre-school provision must be set the benefits of an increased work-force. But the educational developments reported here also have social aspects, as the Scandinavian representatives stressed. The five points of the new Danish Children's Policy, for instance, emphasize that pre-school provision allows for greater equality among the sexes, for freedom of choice and flexibility for the family, and that it allows the social structure of families themselves to be re-defined. As the final Statement agreed by the Ministers itself underlined, in Point 6.1, 'pre-school education policy, including day-care policies, cannot be viewed in isolation from labour market, housing, family allowance and taxation policies'. More than that – and despite the insistent declarations about the real needs and interests of children – it is these other policies which are very largely determining the nature of the evolving educational systems in Europe today. While there is no doubt that the research and development within the pre-school field has influenced the trend towards an earlier start to school, it is largely financial and social pressures which have brought about the present, almost universal, movement towards pre-schooling; a movement which even Iceland has had to take seriously.

This brings us, inevitably, to a consideration of the rights and duties of parents. And here, European states are unanimous in their desire for what is called 'parental participation'. It is, however, not at all clear what education systems actually mean by this term, and there are hints, here and there, that what adminstrators have in mind is a greater declaration of support from families for the essential role of the system. The French enthusiasm for 'the educational team – coherent, efficient and completely orientated towards the child' offers the prospect of a multi-disciplinary approach to education which inevitably carries with it a professionally-dominated hierarchy in which the voice of the parent might become lost. In Italy, by contrast, there is a determination to extend the actual power of parents by offering a form of local control, a development which has its echoes in the United Kingdom playgroup movement but which is unlikely to be followed in those countries where national systems, even if locally administered, are extending their own responsibilities.

In little over a decade, pre-school education has moved in Europe, from being an enthusiasm that was well established in some countries, like France, Belgium and the Netherlands, to becoming an accepted and integrated element of primary schooling. To those who battled for the recognition of the early years of childhood as a unique learning period, such a transformation must seem little short of miraculous. It has become, as the Irish delegate said, 'a fact of educational life'. But to those who are concerned about the relationships that children at this early age have with their family members, with their own homes and their communities, there must remain a degree of ambivalence about such rapid developments. A zest for administrative tidyness and bureaucratic simplicity should not be mistaken for educational profundity. But to those who yearn for a return to an earlier age, and to the fundamentals of the pioneers of pre-schooling, there can be only one response. Europe in the Eighties is a different social milieu and, as the provision it makes for its young citizens changes, so will they.

Statements

AUSTRIA

[...]

I would like not to go over the national statistics of recent years so much as to look at two problems which have been highlighted. These are the questions about the role and the possibilities of parents to participate; and the question of better harmonization, better transfer between pre-schooling and the beginning of primary school, the real school. I think everyone would agree that parents do have a very important role to play in education. In practice, however, it is not made clear what the duties of parents are. I think it is therefore very important that the Council of Europe, in its Committee of Ministers, should point out that parents, and young people who are going to be parents in the future, should bear their responsibilities and should be prepared for these responsibilities. Help should be given to families so that they can really exercise their possible capacities. Perhaps we have not stressed enough the duty of parents to participate in education, and the idea that the capacity for education by parents should be strengthened.

We have tried to do something about this in Austria in adult education, using the mass media to highlight these aspects, with organized seminars for teachers and parents, for nursery school teachers and families, and we have prepared a programme for the education of parents. We have pointed out that, through children's play and in connection with a child's first experiences, parents are laying a very important foundation.

Then we have concentrated on books; a child's first encounter with books is another key-point in his life, and these are experiences where parents can play a very important role, where the family is extremely important. These are areas where the parents should be given support, and where they should be taught how to bear their responsibilities.

The second aspect we have concentrated on is what we call 'Basic stage 1', the beginning of school, the beginning of formal education – and here the problems become quite apparent. Whereas in kindergartens we focus on the family and play and the development of creative activities, in most European countries, as soon as you come to school, the whole system becomes very competitive and far more rigid. Any changes in this concept, any changes in the idea of how teaching should be provided in the population, is simply regarded as being a lowering of the quality of education, as a decline of standards. External requirements continue to be highlighted.

But I see some very hopeful signs that stress that the basic ideas of education need not be changed when you have this transfer to formal education. It should not be such a separate step, but within the school situation, in the way teachers are given their training, such ideas of the preparation of a child for his life should be particularly stressed – this is what should be the dominating idea. If it can be accepted that the idea of promoting development is more decisive than the fulfilment of syllabuses, then the whole concern about compulsory or non-compulsory schooling becomes secondary, and we need no longer feel that this is an important problem, namely, to make sure that children cover a certain programme before they go to school.

BELGIUM

[. . .]

In Belgium today, we are trying to create a basic course in which there is no break between pre-school education and primary education. In fact, I hesitate to use the word 'pre-school', since this idea seems to me to be ambiguous, to say the least. What is more, the accent has, I observe, been put on children between the ages of three and six, whereas we are supposed to be discussing the education of children between the ages of three and eight. While attention should be drawn to the educational needs of children in the three-to-six age group, it has perhaps had the consequence that not enough attention has been paid to the specific needs of primary education for six-to-eight year olds. I would like to add that the 'pre-school' concept as used is not at all appropriate to the situation in Belgium. In fact, the enrolment of children between the ages of two-and-a-half and five has become so important (over 90 per cent at 1 October, 1980), that nursery school attendance can be said to be virtually universal. We intend to table a bill in parliament which defines compulsory schooling; the bill proposes replacing the word 'pre-school' by 'nursery' (*voorschools* becomes *kleuter*), in all the legal texts and regulations. The main feature of this bill is the extension of compulsory schooling both downwards and upwards. In this way we hope that, from 1982 onwards, compulsory schooling will begin at the age of five and continue for eleven consecutive academic years, the first being a year of nursery education.

[. . .]

I see that the idea which emerged when this bill was being drawn up is also expressed in the papers for this Conference, and I quote: 'pre-school education is too valuable in its own right to become merely an extension downwards of present school provision', i.e., primary school. What we want to encourage is the continuation into primary school of the creativity inherent in the best kind of teaching in nursery classes. This demand has been expressed by the educational community, i.e., by teachers and parents.

We are trying to stimulate the active participation of parents in both nursery and primary schools. But, here again, I wonder if we all have the same idea of this active participation of parents? I don't think we do; indeed, I feel that the divergencies are considerable.

Continuity in education, differentiation in the assistance given to children, identifying and helping slow learners, drawing up reports on cooperation between schools and families – this is what we want to achieve in renovating fundamental education. These are the basic aims of the VLO project (i.e., 'modernized primary education'), in the Dutch-language community and of the five-to-eight cycle in the French community.

[. . .]

Unfortunately, there are some problems for which we have not yet found a solution. One is looking after children before and after school hours – a problem which I feel to be extremely important – and another is the training of staff for nursery schools, as distinct from that for the staff of primary schools. In my opinion, these two types of training should be linked in such a way as to ensure continuity of objectives in both sectors.

[. . .]

CYPRUS

[. . .]

Our recent experience of pre-primary education in Cyprus testifies that its general aims can be similar to those of primary education. The new revised curriculum of our schools, which is a product of close cooperation of the school inspectorate, the Union of Teachers, the Pedagogical Academy, the Pedagogical Institute, and parents' associations, is geared to the needs, abilities and potentialities of separate age groups. It takes into account the gradual development of children and the 'teachable periods' or 'critical moments' which characterize childhood. Individual attention, freedom of expression and movement, creativity, flexibility, informality, use of everyday resources, etc., constitute some of our curriculum's main and basic characteristics.

Kindergartens and primary schools in Cyprus come under the jurisdiction of the same educational authority, namely the Department of Elementary Education. Teachers of kindergartens and primary schools have parallel three-year pre-service training courses, at the same Pedagogical Academy. They enjoy equal status and payment, and have equal opportunities for in-service training. This constitutes a unifying factor and guarantees continuity and consistency of teaching approaches and general philosphy of the curriculum, from kindergarten through sixth grade of primary school.

Continuity of teaching methods is unquestionably important. It would be a heavy burden on the young entrants of the primary school to have to adapt to different school situations, especially if they lose individual attention, freedom of movement and expression, and if heavy demands are being made on their scholastic achievement. But a single institutional framework for pre-school and school is not a guarantee for success on continuity. The most important factor is the teacher and the programme.

Public pre-primary education is expanding rapidly all over the island, and hopefully it is expected to reach the children of remote communities in the next few years. But provision should remain noncompulsory, on the principle of individual differences regarding overall maturity, self help and personal independence.

[. . .]

I suggest that this conference should provide the needed incentive for the government of each member State to coordinate the work of the sectors responsible for young children, as the recommendation of the 1969 conference promulgated. Whatever the complexities of the problem in question, the endeavour is worthwhile. Coordination should guarantee reduction of costs, while upgrading quality of provision, by making use of all complementary services to the benefit of childhood.

DENMARK

A debate on the teaching of children under the age of compulsory education is controversial for several reasons. The topic lies on the border between the private and the public sector, and affects family integrity and the parents' sovereign responsibility and competence with regard to raising small children. Societal development has made it increasingly more difficult for families to discharge their responsibilities, and the State therefore shares a responsibility for the children. To this should be added that the State has a clear interest in the possibilities of the rising generation, to develop its physical as well as mental well-being, and to transmit our culture.

[. . .]

Children form part of a family, but they are also citizens in a society, which must therefore care for their special needs. Consequently, in Denmark — as in other countries — there has been a tendency to formulate a *separate* children's policy, which is not, say, social policy, family policy, education policy, labour market policy, or housing policy, but which encompasses all sectors of society. In Denmark, a

Government committee has this spring (1981) set up a list of five basic principles for such a children's policy, which is to form the basis of the political debate on the conditions of life for children. These five principles are in tune with Danish traditions, and with our education-political intentions.

1 A children's policy must be based on equality between sexes, so that the opportunities of mothers are not diminished on account of their children, and in such a way that the children see their parents as being of equal value.
2 A children's policy must be based on endeavours to reach social equality, both for parents and for children.
3 A children's policy must offer options and freedom of choice for parents as well as children; for instance, in terms of occupation, accommodation, schooling and care.
4 A children's policy must have a built-in flexibility so that the many unforeseen events taking place cannot upset the family as a whole.
5 In conclusion, a children's policy must be neutral in relation to the parents' choice of style of cohabitation. It should not be the task of society to direct parents whether singly, or together, whether married or unmarried.

These principles are based on old cultural traditions, as well as a cultural innovation. We must recognize that society does not yet live up to these principles in practice. On the other hand, we can, with satis-faction, state that there is widespread acceptance of these principles in our country.

About 43 per cent of the total work force in Denmark are women, and 80 per cent of mothers with small children have a job. Some 55 per cent of three-to-six year olds now attend kindergartens, and about 90 per cent of the six year olds are in the voluntary pre-school class in the public school. We anticipate a development with practically all children participating in pre-school activities, if their parents wish them to do so.

This creates a good basis for work on planning *vertical continuity*, so that there is agreement between content and methods in pre-school and in the first years at school. It is a prerequisite for this that there is coordination between the social sector, under which kindergartens fall and the school sector, and, in addition, coordination between teacher training courses.

In Denmark we have over the past few years worked on such

planning, which – among other things – will manifest itself in centrally-issued guidance as to coordination of teaching in the pre-school class and in the first two years at school, i.e., a curriculum for children in the age bracket five to eight. In the social sector, educational guidance for kindergartens is being drawn up, and it is my hope that the desired agreement between the sectors can be achieved. It is *not* our intention to fix a curriculum divided into subjects, with a view to an earlier formal education of children, but to respect the pre-school traditions for unrestrained and creative activities, with the point of departure being the needs of the children themselves.

We are especially interested in discussing *horizontal continuity*, i.e., how to create cohesion between home, kindergarten, school, and leisure time. We have unsolved problems, especially about the leisure time of the youngest school children and – to a certain extent – concerning the actual options of parents for an active participation in the work of the pre-school and the school.

Pre-school and leisure-time measures for children are – in addition to their social and cultural significance for the children themselves – necessary prerequisites for equality between sexes. There is therefore a natural connection between the theme of the last session (the education of girls) and the teaching for the children of three to eight.

Of course, I foresee many problems in the theme to be debated. But as they are created by society, i.e., created by people, they can also be solved by human effort. It is significant that in the international cooperation we can exchange experience to be used in the models for solution which we find expedient in our respective national domain.

FINLAND

Industrialization has involved radical changes in children's situations: alienation from the adult world, the working life, nature and demands of adapting to recurrent changes. For millions of children and their families, it has also meant moving away from the native village or town, very often to an entirely new country. All these changes will force us in the 1980s to ask ourselves how international cooperation in different sectors of our economic life affects – and how we want it to affect – the migration flows. In any case, it is probable that international cooperation will to an increasing degree be reflected, possibly in many different ways, in the economic development in all countries, and in particular in manpower and educational affairs.

Today pressure is being exerted on families, arising from the demands of working life, the immediate environment, children's day-care arrangements, housing and consumption, as well as from the prevailing norms and values. The present change also includes an aspect relating to equality between the sexes: women must be equal to men and have the right to a professional education and to take an active part in working life.

The changes have also shaken the family's traditional role as educator and rendered it more difficult. It is true that society has attempted to help the families in their role as educators, i.e., by taking still younger children into the education system. This has been done both by accepting younger age groups and by increasing the number of pre-school places. Although the compulsory school age in most countries outside the Nordic countries begins by the age of six, in many countries over 70 per cent of children of four years old start in pre-school; that is, they are introduced into systematic pre-school education.

Pre-school education ought to complement what children are taught at home, and promote a harmonious development of the children's personality that does not alienate them from their surroundings, but helps them understand and appreciate them better. A pre-school education that is given on the children's own terms forms, together with the home up-bringing, a solid basis for the development of the children's personality and all later education.

From the Finnish point of view all symposia related to pre-school projects have been most helpful. We have in our country felt it to be especially important that attention has been drawn to the improvement of pre-school services for migrant children, as well as for children living in sparsely-populated areas.

The symposia organized in the early 1970s focused attention of the member countries on the organization of a teacher education that would be as high a level as possible, and implemented in close cooperation with the comprehensive school teacher education. This seemed, at the time, to be a very remote goal in many countries, although the significance of cooperation between teacher education at different levels was recognized. The goal, set at the beginning of the last decade, is still very topical. Today attention has to be paid at national level on the development of the pre-school and the comprehensive school, as well as on the pre-conditions for an improvement of the cooperation, through basic and supplementary training, between teachers working in these schools.

FRANCE

[. . .]

At the moment, 81 per cent of children in the two-to-six year age group attend school in France, and for those above the age of four the figure is 100 per cent. As François Mitterand, the President of the Republic, stated recently, we are about to put in hand a plan to open enough nursery schools over a period of several years to make school attendance possible for all children over the age of two, and to reduce the numbers in these classes to 25 pupils. In addition, the actual structure of the nursery school is to be improved (more flexible hours, simpler and more varied organization of sections, improvement of premises, etc.). These changes will be all the more beneficial in that not only the administration of the system, but its organization and operation as well, will be decentralized.

[. . .]

It is now a well-established idea that the education of children does not begin at nursery school, but long before it, and this pre-school period largely conditions the child's whole subsequent school career. It is therefore necessary to develop the educational aspect of the entire system which precedes it: families, crèches, playgroups, etc., and to coordinate its action with all the agencies concerned with children.

[. . .]

It is also necessary to increase the educational work done in the family, particularly by improving the situation of low-income homes which lack the necessary time and means, and by doing more to prepare parents not only to take part directly in their children's education, but also to cooperate with the educational authorities. Parental participation begins in the institutional framework of school associations and councils within which the parents' elected representatives are able to participate directly in the life of the school. This concept of participation should be gradually extended, not only to the problems of the life of the school, but also to its educational action as a whole.

[. . .]

The aim is to build up a true educational team; coherent, efficient, and completely oriented towards the child. In this respect, there are to be more psycho-educational aid groups, taking preventive action against what we tend to speak of as school 'failure'. We will also see that the intitial training given to teachers prepares them for teamwork and participation.

[. . .]

Often, the change from one form of teaching to another is too abrupt: the nursery school is felt to overemphasize play, while primary school very quickly becomes rigid, its methods highly structured. Thus an effort still needs to be made to ease this essential transition, and it must be made at both levels. In the top class of nursery schools children should become accustomed to certain constraints, while the first years of primary schooling should be structured much more gradually, the child's curiosity, imagination and desire to create things being not held back, but, on the contrary, fostered. This task will be greatly facilitated by the fact that, in our country, teachers of nursery and primary schools receive the same training.

[. . .]

WEST GERMANY

[. . .]

In all Lander of the Federal Republic of Germany, compulsory education begins at the age of six in the primary school. Up to that age, children receive most of their education within the family. Education within and by the family, which in our view should have priority at that age, is complemented by the kindergarten. The kindergarten enables children to communicate and experience relationships with others of the same age. This is a task of special importance in view of the sharp drop in the birth rate, which is particularly the case in the Federal Republic of Germany. If both parents are working, or if the mother or the father alone is bringing up the child, then the kindergarten has the additional task of supplementing, and in some cases replacing, family education and care.

There is no legal obligation for children to attend kindergarten. In the Federal Republic of Germany this is a free offer to parents. They can send their children to a kindergarten from the age of three until they enter the primary school. The kindergarten is usually open in the morning and in the afternoon, and where necessary on social grounds – for instance, where both parents are at work – the children can also stay in the kindergarten during the lunch break.

The kindergarten has a pedagogic and a social responsiblity between which there is an interaction. It is true that the kindergarten is also there to ensure that the child does not experience the transition to school as a painful break in his young life, but it is not primarily concerned with preparing children for school. It is not a pre-school in that sense but rather has its own role and significance. This concept of the kindergarten not only endorses the German tradition but has, in the discussion of kindergarten education in our country in recent years, proved to be the dominating view. This is one of the reasons why we have no intention of making kindergarten attendance compulsory.

The organization and financing of kindergartens are governed by the principles of voluntariness, subsidiarity, and plurality. The State has no monopoly of kindergartens. In fact, they are maintained by a variety of institutions, most of them by the so-called 'free' institutions, including in particular the churches and welfare organizations, although these do receive public support. Local authorities only provide kindergarten facilities where the free institutions are not able to do so. The plurality of institutions and the 'subsidiary principle' applying to public kindergartens are of special importance to the situation in Germany.

This concept of the kindergarten is borne out by the opinion that family and kindergarten education should dovetail harmoniously. There should be no conflicts between the two. Consequently, it is not only important that parents should be free in their choice of kindergarten, but also that they should work in close cooperation with the kindergarten staff.

[. . .]

The wider appreciation of the importance of pre-school education in particular has led to the provision of more and better kindergartens over the past ten years. Thus the number of kindergarten places in the Federal Republic of Germany has increased appreciably in recent years. Whereas only 37 per cent of children between the ages of three and six attended kindergarten in 1970, the average today is 75 per cent, and in the case of five year olds as high as 95 per cent. And it should be remembered that this high percentage has been achieved within a system which leaves parents free to choose whether or not to send their children to the kindergarten.

In purely statistical terms, there are almost enough kindergarten places to meet demand, yet some special problems remain. For one thing, there is a trend in Germany away from urban areas. Many people are leaving their homes in the town centres in order to live in a more pleasant, rural environment in the suburbs. This creates a situation where kindergartens in the centre have less and less children attending them, whilst the authorities are obliged to build new kindergartens in the new housing estates − in spite of the declining birthrate. For kindergartens in particular, it is imperative that they should be within easy reach of the home.

Another problem is that in districts where there is a concentration of foreign workers and their families, there are often not enough kindergarten places, because the proportion of children in this section of the population is much greater than that of the German population. There is also the fact, however, that many foreign families are reluctant to send their children to kindergarten. Parents are afraid that if their children are integrated at too early an age with German children they might, at least partly, if not altogether, lose their identity of language, culture and religion. This is an obstacle to efforts to bring German and foreign children together at an early age in order to facilitate their social integration in an informal manner. And I should point out that by 'social integration' we do not mean 'cultural assimilation'.

The kindergarten is not a preparatory school. It is an educational establishment with its own status and its own significance. It provides the child with his first experience of social relationships outside the family, within a group of children. Kindergarten education starts from the principle that children up to the age of five mostly learn about the world at play and in free activity. And to ensure that the primary school, which in Germany admits six-to-nine year olds, does not disturb or cause a complete change in the life of the child, its curriculum is based on the experience gained with the methods used in the kindergarten. This applies particularly in the first two years of primary school, where lessons and teaching are differentiated to suit individual needs, and where the aim is to find the right rhythm between playing and learning. Thus cooperation between kindergartens and primary school teachers can be of great value.

As regards six-to-nine year olds in the primary school, it has been possible in recent years to reduce the teacher/pupil ratio to an average of 25:1. This is partly the result of an increase in the number of teaching posts, but also the fact that the number of pupils has decreased. That, as I said, is the *average* ratio, but I should add that in some cases it is considerably better. The decrease in the primary school population confronts us with major problems, especially in the thinly populated rural areas. But it is particularly important that primary schools should be as near to the children's homes as possible in order to maintain the close links between family and school, and also to spare these children, who are still very young, the trouble of travelling to school by bus. For this reason the teacher/pupil ratio at small country schools is deliberately kept below the average.

It is not only the unusual demographic trend that is causing the present problems facing education policy in the Federal Republic of Germany. True, the bulge years up to the mid-sixties were followed by birthrates which were almost one half less than previous rates, but there are also economic and financial reasons. The building of more primary schools and kindergartens is a good basis for further development, but the present scarcity of resources means that funds have to be used more selectively. Apart from providing a network of primary schools and kindergartens near to children's homes throughout the country, special assistance is needed for handicapped children. In their case, depending on the nature and the extent of their handicap, better and, as far as possible, equal opportunities have to be provided from an early age. Special assistance is, moreover, necessary for the children of foreign workers, not only at school but also at the kindergarten, because we see a great opportunity for these children in particular, with the right kind of assistance, to grow into their new social environment, and in particular to learn the German language at an early age, through play rather than through formal teaching.

[. . .]

GREECE

[. . .]

In Greece, we attach particular importance to pre-school education in order to achieve our aim of equality of both social and cultural opportunity for Greek young people. We believe that all children are entitled to pre-school education, and that is why we are increasing the number of nursery schools, which rose from 3,258 in 1979 to 4,752 in 1980. Today, there are 142,520 children of pre-school age attending nursery schools, whereas five years ago there were only 109,000.

I think it is worth mentioning that in Greece 4,434 of the total number of 4,752 nursery schools are financed by the State, and are entirely under its control, whereas only 313 are private.

[. . .]

At the same time, there are four institutes for training nursery school teachers, who follow a two-year course. It is our plan to increase the length of this course to four years in the near future.

The Ministry of Education is doing its utmost to ensure that there is at least one nursery school, as well as a primary school, in each village, and is paying particular attention to the pre-school education of migrants' children, thereby helping them to maintain links with their country of origin as well as making them familiar with the socio-cultural conditions of the host country.

Because of Greece's geographical configuration, we have made provision for special treatment for children living in sparsely populated areas, such as free transport from home to school, experimental school centres covering several villages, and schools, e.g. on islands, with a very small number of pupils.

[. . .]

HOLY SEE

[. . .]

Pre-school education cannot be made compulsory. Even if it is to the child's advantage to have attended nursery school for one or two years before entering primary school, it would not be possible to begin compulsory schooling at the age of three or four, and extended schooling already places a heavy burden on young people. Moreover, early compulsory schooling would destroy the special quality and value of teaching at that level, and turn kindergartens into schools, which would be a great loss.

Rather than imposing pre-school attendance on children from the age of three, it would seem preferable to make it possible, through some social organization, for the parent wanting to stay at home to raise his or her young children to do so without the family's budget suffering. Perhaps a wage could be paid to mothers staying at home, and the years they spend there could count towards their total period of employment.

[. . .]

IRELAND

[. . .]

Apart from the difficulty in any discussion on the educational provision to be made for pre-school education arising from the age range of the children involved, and the varying stages of development, there are also the considerations and pressures of a social nature which tend to obtrude to such an extent as to threaten the feasibility of discussion based on purely educational objectives.

It may, of course, be rightly claimed that the educational system cannot be isolated and considered apart from the social circumstances in which it operates. Such an argument has validity in relation to the whole process from pre-primary school up to university level and beyond into adult education. Even so, care has to be taken at all stages to preserve the fundamental basis and intrinsic values of what is generally understood by education, and at least equal care should be taken to seek to appreciate as clearly as possible ·what aspect of pre-school provision for child-care we mean when we refer to educational provision and the extent of the need for it.

It would seem at times that there may be a tendency to approach this matter from the standpoint of: 'my mind is made up — don't attempt to confuse me with facts'. The pressure is there to make certain provision for children outside the home, perhaps for their whole waking hours for almost every day of the week, and it is considered for various reasons that the educational system should become involved in the process.

It is difficult to resist the temptation to consider that even if it were to be established scientifically — whatever that may mean in educational terms of modern day methods — that pre-school provision for children at too early an age was actually harmful, that pressure for its provision would still continue.

It is in these circumstances that it may be suggested that Ministers of Education should always insist that proposals in the pre-school area should be carefully assessed for their educational contribution to the child's development. They would be concerned to do so in consideration of the expenditure involved and the alternative use to which scarce financial resources might be put, to the care that is called for to ensure that children should be protected from the dangers associated with experimentation and to the avoidance of disappointments which could follow from unrealistic expectations not being realized. They would be encouraged in such resolve by the experience of so many experiments in various countries over an extended period of years.

Disappointment has been experienced from the failure of Head Start programmes in the U.S. to make a sustained significant contribution to the subsequent success of pupils in primary schools. The experience has been the same in the case of similar projects in other countries, including the Irish/Van Leer Foundation Rutland Street project in Dublin. It is difficult to be very sanguine about the more recent claims that a link, direct or indirect, can be established between pre-school experience at three-to-four years and subsequent progress of pupils in their teens. It seems to me that there are many imponderables which may occur in the meantime to be taken into account.

The particular point which I would wish to make in this connection relates to the concept of equal educational opportunity for all. Pre-school education becomes more expensive as the provision for it is extended, as — in the case of Ireland — identical arrangements for training of teachers in pre-school and primary schools and identical conditions of service and levels of salary apply, and class size is reduced. Does the question need to be asked: would such additional expenditure as an input at some later stage of the educational process give better results? It could certainly be applied more uniformly, i.e. as between children in urban and rural areas.

Nevertheless, pre-school education is a fact of educational life and we should seek to ensure that it achieves the greatest benefit possible for the greatest number of children who may be in a position to avail themselves of it. [. . .] One of the problems relates to the transition from pre-school to primary school and the new arrangements being introduced in the Netherlands. I do not claim any special credit for Ireland in that the system being introduced now in the Netherlands was the one which grew up – or grew down, whichever way you look at it – in Ireland. Provision had existed for many years for voluntary enrolment of children from four years of age in infant schools or in the infant classes of primary schools. The percentage of the age group enrolled was low for many years, but in recent years has increased very substantially.

At the same time, during the Seventies we introduced an integrated child-centred programme for all classes in the primary school in substitution for the more subject-centred programme which had obtained previously. It may be, accordingly, that I may be able to issue a word of comfort, as well as a word of caution, to our Dutch colleagues. The child-centred approach, instead of being swamped by the more traditional approach of the primary school as hitherto followed, took on for all classes of the primary school. Alas, the problem did not disappear entirely; it emerged at the stage of transition from primary to secondary school. A Committee was established by the Minister for Education in 1978 to examine and report on the problems involved. It has just reported – in the week in which the Dáil (our Parliament), was dissolved and a General Election called! [. . .]

ITALY

Pre-school education has grown constantly, in my country, during the last 15 years, in numbers as well as in academic efforts and legislative action. The central government's policies have constantly aimed at expanding attendance in a sector like that of nursery education, which had hitherto been entirely entrusted to voluntary organizations or to local authorities.

Let me quote a few significant figures covering the past 25 years: in 1957-58, nursery school pupils totalled 1 million 80 thousand. Ten years later, in 1967-68, they totalled 1 million 409 thousand. In 1977-78 attendance had risen to 1 million 822 thousand, and last year it further rose slightly to 1 million 830 thousand.[. . .]

These data are encouraging, even though they are considered little more than an indication of a trend towards more satisfactory goals. What counts most is perhaps the fact that nursery education in Italy has lost many of its 'care' and 'custody' features that used to characterize it in the past, and is acquiring definite educational characteristics in an effort to implement the 'right of education' which, by general consent, children are entitled to.

In other words, pre-school has acquired an educational shape of its own, thus becoming part of the 'basic education' system, together with elementary and middle school.

While, however, satisfactory results have been achieved in setting educational goals, several obstacles still make it difficult to assess precisely the role of pre-school *vis-à-vis* the traditional area of primary school on the one hand and the family and community environment on the other; a problem which has been evidenced internationally. [. . .]

In Italy, in particular, there exists an additional difficulty, caused by the tripartite nature of nursery education, which is divided into state-, private- and, to a minor extent, local authority-run schools.

This is one more reason for my country's particular interest in this meeting, in view of the response that is likely to come to certain basic questions posed in the discussion paper:

1 the continuity of the educational process in pre-school and primary school ('vertical continuity')
2 the relationship between pre-school, family and local community (horizontal continuity)
3 last, but not least, teacher training.

[. . .]

As far as my country is concerned, two priorities stand out: a) the need for nursery education to be made available to the whole age group three-to-five year olds (about half a million new places are to be provided, most of them in the South) and b) the possible adoption of one single institutional framework for the three-to-eight age group. The latter, in my opinion, ought in any case to be devised as a flexible 'route', capable of closely linking together nursery and first-cycle primary education.

From a strictly educational viewpoint, this initial schooling stage ought to foster the acquisition of basic language skills and of value systems, and should involve such cognitive processes as are required for a balanced vertical curriculum. On the other hand, it should also be capable of inspiring feelings of confidence and security on the part of children, thus helping them to acquire emotional stability.

The core of 'vertical continuity' ought to consist in a unified model designed to provide a well-balanced curriculum in which the teaching contents of the first stage of primary school are linked and coordinated with the earlier provisions of pre-school pedagogy. Any such connection should also be considered in the light of possible changes in the institutional arrangement of present day basic education.

In particular, a unified three-to-eight model would imply a reshuffling of the present organization of nursery and elementary school systems. It is no doubt an interesting hypothesis, but it requires further careful consideration and analysis in view of the consequences that might derive to the other branches of compulsory education and also for the political, cultural, labour as well as administrative implications which any major reform of this kind may involve.

Other important issues, more or less directly connected with this project, are the object of lively discussion in Italy at present. They involve, among other things, the issue of the extension of compulsory schooling, for which three alternatives are offered, namely a) lowering of compulsory primary school attendance to five; b) lowering of compulsory schooling to five as at a) above, with children continuing to attend nursery school, and c) reduction of primary school period to four years, with consequent raising of school leaving age to 15 (i.e. in coincidence with the inception of legal working age), so as to include the two years of initial cycle of upper secondary education.

The right of pre-school children to acquire better learning skills, together with more varied, socially valuable experiences than those afforded within the family, and to enjoy educational opportunities which may be lacking in the home, is emphasized by those advocating the lowering of compulsory school age, who also stress the need for educational institutions to compensate for the social and cognitive disadvantages of the children from deprived backgrounds.

An opposite view is held by those who believe that early schooling might adversely affect the child's right 'to be a child' and might turn him into too early a 'pupil', forcing him to spend long hours in school, away from his own family and from the experiences of the home.

Still, in terms of 'horizontal continuity', which has been rightfully given as much importance as 'vertical continuity' in my country, at present a bill is pending before the Chamber of Deputies, after winning the approval of the Senate, which provides for the extension to nursery education of the regulations governing parental participation at all educational levels. [. . .]

Further significant developments are likely to follow this initial, formal opening to the family in the direction emphasized by the supporters of the so-called 'écoles des parents'. Councils and assemblies may, in fact, foster the exchange of experiences, suggestions and plans to the advantage of the services that governmental nursery schools are called upon to render at the initial educational stage. Similar connections have been established with local communities. The decentralization process carried out during the past decade has entrusted local authorities with the performance of important educational duties in such fields as school building and health and sanitation.[. . .]

Finally, with regard to teacher training, legislation in force since 1974 requires that prospective nursery school teachers attend higher education degree courses either at university or at other higher education institutions. In view of this provision[. . .] common teacher training programmes could be devised for both nursery and first-cycle primary teachers, thus also facilitating closer links between first- and second-cycle basic education. Along this line, an initial two-year training period in common for all prospective nursery and primary teachers could be arranged, to be followed by a further two-year period of training offering special courses in a common-core curriculum for the three-to-eight model teachers.

ICELAND

Compulsory education in Iceland is stipulated by an act of parliament: children have to attend school from the autumn of the year they reach the age of seven. The same act stipulates the following about pre-schools:

> Local councils may permit comprehensive schools to establish classes for six-year-old children, or five-to-six-year-old children, if the ministry approves their plans, accommodation and equip-

ment. Pre-schools are budgeted in the same way as comprehensive schools. The teachers are expected to possess recognized teaching certificates and their conditions of appointment and salary are the same as those of junior school teachers. Teachers with special additional qualifications as pre-school teachers have priority claim to appointment. The schools are entitled to employ nursery teachers and other specially qualified staff, as required. They are employed and paid by the same authority as the teachers, and their salaries are in accordance with negotiated or arbitrated settlements.

Comprehensive schools are permitted to allocate part of their premises to organize pre-school classes. Private pre-schools are not permitted without the consent of the District School Supervisor concerned.

[. . .]

There are 216 comprehensive schools in the country, with pupils from six to sixteen: of these, 182 contain the youngest age groups. The average number of pupils in each school is about 194. Of the 216 schools, there are 70 with more than the average number of pupils, the biggest enrolling 1,217. This shows that there are a great number of small schools in the country districts, the smallest with only five pupils.

In Reykjavik, the most populous district, there are about 23 children on average in each class of seven-to-eight year old children, whereas in rural districts there are often only a few children in each grade, so vertical classes are common. In most urban areas, pupils are divided into groups according to age.

In most schools two (sometimes even three), classes use the same classroom; one in the morning, the other in the afternoon. In most schools the teacher teaches all subjects, except in the larger schools, where there are specialist teachers for P.E. and music and occasionally for art and craft.[. . .]

The introductory section of the curriculum expects children to be active participants in the learning process and to gain direct experience through observation and experimentation.

Teaching methods in the lower grades have in many schools undergone a change from the traditional methods where the teacher supplied information to more pupil-orientated activities with the teacher serving as a guide and director of work in a warm and stimulating learning environment.[. . .]

Pre-schools were established by all comprehensive schools in Reykjavik in 1970, and the years that followed saw a steady increase in the number of pre-schools outside Reykjavik. Today there are 4,032 children or 96.7 per cent of all six-year-old children (born 1974), attending pre-schools.

The pre-schools are, in all instances, run by comprehensive schools and on their premises. They often suffer from overcrowding, as they were not taken into account when those school-buildings designed before 1970 were planned. In spite of being a part of the comprehensive school, the pre-school follows different guidelines, for example, in number of lessons, teaching materials, and equipment.

The number of lessons available depends upon local conditions, but the ministry stipulates the maximum. The average class size for the country is 17, excluding schools that have vertical classes.

According to the law, pre-school teachers are to possess a teacher's certificate, but the schools may employ 'children's nurses and other qualified staff'.

In 1980-81, 226 teachers were working in the pre-schools; of these, 173 had a teacher's certificate, 30 were children's nurses, and 23 had other qualifications. Of the 226, only 51 had attended courses for pre-school teachers. Such courses were held by the Reykjavik Education District Authority in the first years of the pre-schools.

As they are not a part of the compulsory school system, the Ministry of Education has not taken any policy or curriculum decisions for the pre-schools. Their work is therefore dependent upon the decision of each educational district, or the comprehensive school concerned.

Only one district office in Reykjavik has provided the pre-schools with guidelines and some materials.

The objectives of the pre-schools in Reykjavik feature four main components:

1 adjusting the child to school
2 bridging the period in the child's life between play and school
3 providing the children with an opportunity to develop physically, emotionally, socially, and intellectually
4 preventive work.

In the first half of the school year the main emphasis is on education which strengthens muscular coordination, develops the senses of hearing and sight, increases command of speech and helps social adjustment. The work consists of painting, drawing, moulding and games involving movement, music, drama, etc. This work is also related to preparatory exercises in reading, writing and mathematics. In the second half of the school year, more emphasis is placed on reading and arithmetic. As a result of this shift, there is little scope for varied work because each day of schooling is very short (a maximum of two hours a day).

Elsewhere pre-school teachers have relied upon materials designed for the first and second grades, or they have prepared material themselves. Generally speaking, there is an emphasis on preparing the children for reading, writing and mathematics by the use of arts and games.

In November 1980, the Ministry of Education appointed a commission to investigate the problems facing pre-schools. The commission was to make policy proposals and recommend what steps should be taken in the near future. The commission found that they were unable to separate the pre-schools completely from the first grades of the comprehensive schools and in their work they looked upon the pre-school as 'school commencement' or part of the continuous education of six-to-eight year old children. Particular consideration was given to the position of the youngest children, with regard to the ever increasing rate at which both parents go out to work. The commission's conclusions are due soon. [. . .]

LUXEMBOURG

[. . .]

The subject of discussion at this Conference is one of great current importance in our country, and we are at present working on a fundamental reform of primary education. The Ministry of Education has set up a permanent commission on the subject, which is responsible for studying the aims, structures, programmes and methods of primary education.

[. . .]

In the Discussion Paper prepared by the Committee of Senior Officials, emphasis was rightly placed on the important mission of pre-school education as 'a way of ensuring greater equality of opportunity by providing a rich and stimulating environment for all children on an equal footing during the years of rapid intellectual development before the start of compulsory school'. The paper also rightly stresses that 'to ignore the needs of children from deprived backgrounds for help from the earliest stages would amount to perpetuation of that deprivation'. It has been a goal of those responsible for education in the Grand Duchy of Luxembourg to provide pre-school education for all.

[. . .]

In 1974, when attendance at kindergartens was optional, the rate had already reached 89 per cent for four year olds and 95 per cent for five year olds.

In the interests of the 5 per cent of five year olds who did not attend kindergartens, and who were among those who needed most to do so (particularly migrants' children and children from underprivileged social classes), attendance was made compulsory for five year olds in 1976; all children in this age group must now go to kindergartens, while for four year olds attendance is still optional.

[. . .]

It should be borne in mind that there are many foreign children in our country currently attending pre-school classes; the proportion was 33 per cent in 1976, 37.8 per cent in 1978 and the upward trend is continuing, since the birthrate among Luxembourg families is considerably lower than that among foreign families. This year in the city of Luxembourg, where more than one-third of the country's population lives, the proportion of foreign children in pre-school education is over 57 per cent. The problems this raises for our pre-school education can be imagined. We have to redefine our objectives, content and working methods for these children, to facilitate their integration into the school community and their transition to primary school, mainly through learning the national language.

[. . .]

The statistics for failure in the first years of primary school show that repeats are particularly frequent during the first years. It was to remedy this state of affairs that the government made one year of pre-school education compulsory for five year olds and decided that primary schooling would begin at six with considerably reduced class size. In our country, the average number of children per class in the first year of study is 16.5, which is an extremely good figure. In the first six years of study as a whole, the average is 17.7 pupils.

[...]

With our present structure, there is, unfortunately, a great leap between pre-school and primary education, and primary school is cut up into distinct chronological divisions, with the result that children are asked to learn faster than is possible for most of them. Structures should be made more flexible, particularly at the beginning of schooling, when children should be prepared for basic learning. The determining factors should be neither age nor the numbers of years of school attendance, but rather the possibilities of each pupil. It is desirable that each child should learn to read during the first year of study, for example, but by no means indispensable that all be able to read at the end of the year.

[...]

The use of active teaching methods and compensatory measures at the beginning of schooling may help to improve the situation. A structure without annual stages (as in Great Britain), might also mean greater individualization in teaching. With this in mind, the Ministry of Education has recommended that local authorities treat the first two years at school as a single teaching unit.

[...]

The central problem of teaching in Luxembourg is our bilingualism. All Luxembourg children learn at least two major cultural languages, neither of which they regard as their mother tongue, from their first years at primary school. The study of German is begun in the first year, French in the second.

The second central problem is that of the presence of many foreign children. In 1979, 32 per cent of all children enrolled in primary education were foreign, but in some areas and towns the percentages are even higher. The integration of these foreign children raises problems which are difficult to solve, particularly since, because of our bilingualism, 75 per cent of the primary school timetable is devoted to languages, arithmetic and religious education, and only 25 per cent to other activities, for example, introducing the natural sciences and sport.

[...]

Schools and teachers in Luxembourg therefore face problems which are difficult to solve, and that is why I attach so much importance to the reform of training for pre-school and primary teachers, which is soon to be extended to three years of post-secondary study and which includes the institutionalization of in-service training for working teachers. In my opinion, a good training as well as the introduction of in-service training geared to teachers' needs are essential to an improvement in the quality of our schools.

The problem of the level of training of pre-school and primary teachers has been raised on several occasions. In our country, pre-school and primary teachers are trained to the same level, and although their training is not identical, there is close liaison. Student teachers choose to train for either pre-school or primary education, but some courses and training periods are common to both; for example, those who wish to teach in pre-school education must do some of their teaching practice in primary schools.

Another rather serious problem in our country concerns the recruitment of student teachers. At the moment, admission is based on secondary school-leaving examination marks, but unfortunately — or fortunately — we have six times as many candidates as there are vacant posts. This method of selection is therefore no longer satisfactory, and I would like to know what methods are used in other countries with similar selection problems.

The Discussion Paper for this Conference also mentioned encouraging a better balance between the sexes in the staffing of pre-school and primary education. About 60 per cent of the teachers working in primary education are men, and 40 per cent are women, and we are trying to maintain this percentage in selecting new applicants. In pre-school education, the percentage of women teachers is over 99 per cent, and although we would like to have more men, applicants unfortunately are very few and far between.

In conclusion, I would like to mention briefly the relationship between family and school, a problem which is of major importance especially in the education of three-to-eight year olds. This problem has not been solved satisfactorily in our country.[...]

Our parents' associations at primary level have had no legal status in the past, either nationally or locally. Their aims, rights and duties are not clearly defined, and we shall try to remedy this. Pre-school and primary schools are organized by the local authorities and must be approved by the Minister of Education. The local body of control and supervision is the 'school commission', the members of which are appointed by the local authorities. Parents do not have the right to appoint a representative to this body, and the only representative of the teaching staff is a delegate with consultative status. This is why I intend to change the law and turn the school commissions into genuine tripartite bodies on which the local authorities, parents and teachers would be equal partners.

Up to now, we have never had headmasters or heads of establishments in primary school education centres, and we have tried gradually to improve direct contacts between parents and teachers by introducing an information meeting for parents at the beginning of the academic year, holding regular meetings and consultations for parents, setting up regional counselling services with the assistance of a team of psychologists, educationalists, teachers, doctors and social assistants. This service is mainly for children with mental, physical or behavioural problems or learning difficulties. Its aims are to identify such children at an early stage, give them educational help, keep in close contact with their parents and counsel them effectively.[. . .]

NETHERLANDS

[. . .]

In a country such as the Netherlands, where for many years nearly all children have attended nursery school from the age of four, there is no doubt that the integration of pre-school and primary education constitutes the best means of ensuring 'vertical continuity', and it is for this reason that the Dutch Chamber of Deputies recently adopted a new basic education act, instituting a type of education which is to apply to virtually all children from around four years old up to the age of 12.

Compulsory schooling would therefore begin one or two years earlier than at present. This being the case, 'pre-school' education in the Netherlands, as for example in Belgium, is limited to three year olds. The logical result of the integration of pre-school and primary education to which I have just referred will be integrated training for all the teachers involved. In developing it, every effort will be made to preserve the working methods employed in what was formerly pre-school education.

The Netherlands are fully aware of the risk inherent in this integration, i.e. a predominance of the traditional approach to primary education, in which the emphasis is on the material to be learned. Over the decades, pre-school education, on the other hand, has evolved an approach and methods of its own, the value of which is unquestionable and unquestioned. It will also be necessary for former nursery school teachers to have the same status as primary school teachers within the basic school, including, for example, the same entitlement to take part in the management of the basic school. Personally, I am all in favour of this.

Nevertheless, I feel I must stress that the integration of what has previously been called pre-school and primary education does not constitute a reform in itself, but is merely one element in the overall process of renewal within basic education. In my opinion, the new basic education should, for example, help greatly in breaking away from the sex-based stereotypes which limit the opportunities of girls and women in education and later in social and economic life. In addition, the aims leading to the establishment of basic education are: firstly, respect for the child's individuality and identity, which are to be taken into account as much as possible; secondly, increased educational opportunities; and thirdly, improved facilities to enable schools to take in handicapped and problem children.

Basic education will be for children between the ages of four and 12. While these age limits, particularly the lower one, have been determined by historical development rather than educational criteria, it can nevertheless be said that the emphasis begins to shift, around three or four, away from the child-minding function towards the educational function. What is more, if day-care facilities are made generally available for children under four we may well find ourselves confronted with a new problem, i.e. the transition from this stage to the new basic education. We must begin to think about this problem at once. In the interest of equality of opportunities, child-minding and educational facilities for the very young child are of capital importance.

[. . .]

The new Dutch basic education act requires compulsory schools to draw up each year, in consultation with the representatives of the pupils' parents, a school action plan showing, in particular, how contacts with parents are maintained.

In the last few years a large number of projects have been carried out in preparation for the new integrated basic school. It is still too soon to judge all the results of these. Perhaps, in due course, we shall have to take even more far-reaching steps. I feel that the school, as Mr van der Eyken suggests in his report, must continue to develop until it becomes an educational centre for both children and parents, cooperating with the adult education authorities and other socio-cultural institutions. Such a development offers the best possibility for fruitful comprehension and cooperation between parents and schools. This is particularly important for migrants' children. In the Netherlands, their right to preserve their own identities is recognized and fully supported.

[. . .]

Education is expensive, and money doesn't grow on trees. What is more, when there is a decline in prosperity the question who should pay for what becomes more acute. I feel that so long as pre-school education is not universal or compulsory it is fair to ask parents to make a contribution, in proportion to their income. The great difficulty of establishing a cost-benefit analysis where educational equipment is involved is no secret, but the need for such analysis is greater today than ever before and not only for pre-school facilities. Perhaps we might reconsider this problem in a European context.

What is certain when we speak of extending educational facilities for young children is that it is absolutely vital to fix priorities. I personally feel that preference must be given in public expenditure for pre-school education to the children of single-parent families, migrant families and the socially under-privileged.

[. . .]

NORWAY

In the last few generations, the countries of Europe have experienced very rapid changes. These changes have to a large extent altered the conditions for family life in general, as well as the immediate surroundings within which the family operates.

On the other hand, the increasing standard of living has enabled most families to provide their children with economic security, and better educational opportunities have made it possible for parents to give their children a healthy and stimulating upbringing.

On the other hand, family structures have changed, so that parents, more than before, stand alone in that part of the upbringing of their children which takes place in the home. There are fewer and fewer families where grandparents or older brothers and sisters can help the parents in looking after, and raising, the young. But no one today can draw a small circle around their own life and state that whatever occurs outside of this circle is of no concern to them. Even at a tender age, the child must prepare itself for being able to master a future with great challenges and changes in family life, economic life, and societal conditions.

The situation thus seems to be that the responsibilities which families have in the upbringing of children is more comprehensive and demanding than ever before.

It is, furthermore, no longer the case that the question of which parent should have the main responsibility for the upbringing of the children is self-evident. Not all mothers take upon themselves, more or less automatically, the sole responsibility for the care and development of their children. In more and more families, the question of child-raising is one to which a solution must be found by mutual agreement between the parents.

Parents are increasingly looking to society for support in the raising of small children — much in the same way they now are supported in the raising of school age children. If nursery schools are to give a positive contribution to the upbringing of children and their adaption to society, they must develop a distinctive character based on the special needs and possibilities of young children. Through being together and playing in groups children learn to interact, to cooperate and to solve common tasks.

Contact with people outside the nursery school can enhance children's ability to involve themselves with other people and make them more tolerant of people or groups of people different from themselves.

Economic recessions often lead to reductions in the public services. It is in my opinion important that a society experiencing economic problems *does not* reduce those programmes which, to a large extent, help prepare the coming generation to endure and overcome difficult living conditions. It is in times of hardship that societal solidarity is put to the most extreme tests, and cooperation and creativity are the most important societal resources. The good start which children can get in nursery schools can therefore prove to be an important investment in making the future more secure.

There is, in the Nordic countries at present, an intensive debate on the goals and contents of nursery schools. Important questions have been raised regarding such matters as: the relationship between responsibility of the parents and the contribution from nursery schools in the raising of children; the relationship between caretaking, socialization, and education in nursery schools; the role of nursery schools in the ethical guidance of the children; and the relationship between professional and non-professional personnel in child care.[. . .]

Instead of lowering the school starting age from seven to six, Norwegian education authorities have considered it useful to evaluate more closely the pedagogical aspects of pre-school and primary school facilities. On this background pilot projects have been launched with a view to establish integrated educational measures for children from four to nine years of age. Facilities for children from four to nine years of age are actually administered by three ministries, that is, the Ministry of Consumer Affairs and Government Administration, the Ministry of Social Affairs and the Ministry of Education. It is thus necessary to establish a close cooperation between these ministries.

The reasons for introducing programmes for mixed age groups may perhaps be questioned. Norway has a long tradition in running schools with pupils of various ages within the same class. During the last ten years Norwegian kindergartens have also been trying various forms of age grouping and gained some experience with groups, including children from three to seven years of age.

Studies carried out within the fields of anthropology and social psychology have shown that the socialization of children is easier in mixed age groups than in groups which are homogenous in terms of age. In the process of the social adaptation during childhood older children play an important role in bringing cultural values and traditions to the younger ones.

We also know that school children solve problems far better in mixed age groups than in groups with children of equal age. It is further presumed that in an age-mixed group the group will in itself serve as a protector of the younger. Older children will help the younger. We also believe that groups composed of children of various ages may reduce tendencies to competition among the children. In groups of this kind each individual child may easily find playmates on an equal level. The child is not necessarily encouraged to compare himself with other children of the same age, and possibly compete with them.

If we look at this project from the point of view of special education, it gives — in our judgement — far greater pedagogical possibilities than in classes and groups with children of the same age.[. . .]

Also, in these projects, parents will participate as responsible co-workers. By giving the parents influence and responsibility, we hope to be better able both to meet the needs of each family and to adapt the programmes to the conditions of the various local communities.[. . .]

In view of the present economic situation, however, the most important task in the years to come will be to secure sufficient financial resources to maintain and further develop pre-schools and primary schools of good quality. This is a challenge that all the member countries have in common.

PORTUGAL

[. . .]

In Portugal, we are experiencing a very important phase of development of our pre-school education system.

Under a policy of favouring equality of opportunity, our legislation aims to foster harmonious child development while at the same time lowering barriers of social and cultural differences on access to the school system. We endeavour to encourage the entire development of the child as a useful and necessary member of the spiritual, moral, cultural, social and economical progress of the community.

It is the task of the Ministry of Education and Science to lay down the general rules and orientation of pre-school education, and to stimulate projects in close consultation with families and other interested groups. In doing so, we are generating educative praxis with a great degree of flexibility that takes the economic, social and cultural realities of the country into account.

The variety of services and the evolution of educational concepts are pressing the Department of Education to an ever wider and stronger role in promoting local initiatives.

In the last two years we have doubled, every year, the total number of kindergartens. In this process of expansion we are particularly interested in the creation of pre-school education facilities in the rural areas; areas where the partnership of the community and the educator are particularly important. There exist neither sophisticated buildings nor equipment. There are not large numbers of children or staff. But there exists an enriching experience.

So we are attempting to introduce flexible models of intervention, adapted to the everyday needs of children and their families, and not complicated by deep speculations of either a pedagogic or didactic nature.[. . .]

SPAIN

[. . .]

Our general education act, which dates back to 1970, treated pre-school education in essentially the same way as the recommendations of the first Council of Europe symposium on this subject in Versailles. We in Spain are now attaching greater importance to pre-school education, and there are many reasons for this, among them the larger numbers of women entering the working world, real commitment to the principle of equality of opportunity, and, above all, the decisive importance of educational activity during this period of childhood, as illustrated by the latest psychological and educational research.

However, the need to establish overall priorities for education and the traditional budgetary difficulties of Ministries of Education, now further aggravated by the economic crisis, have forced us to concentrate our attention on certain age groups. Our first objective was school attendance by all six-to-13 year olds, since that is the period of compulsory education in Spain. Having achieved this objective, our aim is now to provide completely free education for all pupils in compulsory schooling and the gradual inclusion of four and five year olds in pre-school education. At the moment, 80 per cent of children in this age group attend school, and we hope to achieve total attendance during the next three years. At the same time, we are also making progress towards the second goal of free schooling.

[. . .]

Children do not change abruptly at the age of six merely because they enter primary school and leave behind them the nursery school or kindergarten. On this point, the Spanish Ministry of Education has taken into account the recommendations of the Versailles symposium and, in 1976, began a comprehensive study with a view to the coordination of pre-school and primary education. The results, presented at the Bournemouth symposium, have been applied experimentally for the past three years. Finally, this year, we decided on the definitive organization of schools, beginning next year. The new system includes a two-year initial cycle which corresponds exactly to pre-school education. By means of this coordination, the same objectives are covered in both educational sectors, and constantly adjusted to the pupils' levels of maturity.

We have introduced minimum standards which pupils must attain at the end of the pre-school sector, and then at the end of the initial cycle of primary education, thus giving parallel results. In this way there is no break between pre-school education and beginning of primary schooling, but rather a continuity in objectives and methodology.

[. . .]

In Spain we are trying to coordinate the related activities of the Ministries of Labour, Health, and Social Security with those of the Ministry of Education. [. . .] This is just one example to show that educational policy should be supplemented by other social measures, particularly in the fields of employment, housing social security and even taxation.

This effort to harmonize the child's life in his family with pre-school education and with a rational use of public money has led us to set up some experiments in pre-school education at home with the cooperation of the parents themselves, under the guidance of teachers and specialized staff who supply appropriate teaching materials.

[. . .]

In conclusion, I would like to make some comments on the great problem of teachers. In Spain, the teachers responsible for pre-school education have the same basic qualifications as those who teach in primary schools. We have nevertheless introduced a special course for pre-school education, which teachers can take either at the national university for distance education, or directly in teacher training colleges. This method was instituted in 1977, and since the course lasts three years, we are only beginning to see the first fruits of it now. It is obvious that in order to be effective, the reform in the curricula for primary and pre-school education introduced in Spain must be accompanied by a reform in the curricula of the teacher training colleges.

[. . .]

SWEDEN

[. . .]

In Sweden, as well as in many other countries in Europe and abroad, we now have a situation where an ever-growing proportion of the children who go to the regular, compulsory school have previous experience of 'pre-school', that is, of attending a day nursery or a kindergarten. Obviously, this development makes it desirable to have close ties between the pre-school and the regular school. For the individual child, the activity should stand out as a single unit even if two types of activity are involved, perhaps each with its own governing authority. We know, however, that in many countries there are big differences between pre-schools and regular schools in their activities. These differences are partly due to the fact that, in some countries, the official responsibility for the two school types is divided. The pre-school belongs to the social services sector, whereas the regular school, of course, forms part of the educational sector. To my mind, however, the question of governing responsibility is secondary. More important, the differences between pre-school and regular school can surely be explained in terms of different objectives and traditions. The regular school usually has a constrained activity, that is controlled by official curricula which may specify objectives even for every single school grade.

By contrast, the pre-school is often not subject to the same constraints, but affords greater scope for initiative at the local level. According to several Swedish studies of how the two institutional types differ in their modes of working, the pre-school gives the children more leeway to exercise their own initiatives, while in the regular school there is a tendency for the children to engage more frequently in common activities and under guidance aimed at the whole group.

Another difference is that most of what is done in the pre-school takes the form of teamwork between the adult staff members, whereas the tradition in the regular school is for each teacher to work independently with her own class. I think these conclusions also hold for other countries to a great extent.

Hence there are substantial differences between pre-schools and regular schools when it comes to working methods and content. As a result many children feel that the regular school does not follow through naturally on the pre-school. The desirable continuity of the child's development is disrupted. For many pupils, starting school can be a negative experience, full of tensions and insecurity.

Given this background, there are compelling reasons which argue for taking greater pains to bring the pre-school and regular school closer to one another. In my opinion such intensified collaboration must be based on a similar view of the development and needs of children. In his report, especially Chapter 3 'The needs of the competent child', Mr van der Eyken has laid a very good foundation for this approach. Here I should especially like to single out the gratifying attention paid to what Sweden is doing to combat corporal punishment as well as other forms of physical and mental punishment. We can never hope to have a school based upon humanistic and democratic ideals if at the same time we allow the school and the rest of society to use methods of upbringing children which directly conflict with these ideals. I hope that the positive experiences we have gained in Sweden (and these are also described in the report), of our 20-year ban on corporal punishment in school can spur other countries to start discussions about abolishing physical and mental punishment of children.

A similar view on the development and needs of children should enhance the feasibility of bringing pre-schools and regular schools closer to each other in their working modes and methods. The goal here should be to make the transition from one school type to the other so flexible as to permit making allowance for the individual maturity and qualifications of every single child. We know that a child's developmental age may differ considerably from its biological age. By the time they start school, children may be several years apart in their developmental levels, and there need be nothing abnormal about this. A child's developmental level may also shift in various respects — intellectually, socially, physically, etc. A more flexible transition from pre-school to regular school should be able to take such differences between children into account, and in that way give every single child better opportunities to develop favourably.

SWITZERLAND

[. . .]

In Switzerland, it is the cantons which are responsible for public education, with the exception of a few provisions relating to physical education, apprenticeships, the secondary school-leaving certificate and the training of students at advanced technical colleges. In the absence of a Ministry of Education, after working separately for decades, the cantons have now felt the need to harmonize their legislation in the interests of education. An 'international concordat on school coordination' was approved by the Federal Council on 14 December 1970 and submitted to each canton for approval, but not all have acceded to it thus far; it provides the general outline for recommendations applying to all cantons and covering, in particular, model curricula, common teaching materials, freedom of transfer between equivalent schools, entry into the secondary cycle, recognition at cantonal level of school-leaving certificates and diplomas awarded for equivalent study, uniform designation of educational levels and types of schools, and equivalent training for teachers.

The concordat is mainly concerned with the period of compulsory schooling between the ages of six and 15 and subsequent studies leading to the 'Certificat de maturité', but does not deal with the pre-school period, undoubtedly because of the enormous disparity to be found in Switzerland at this level. In some cantons, children are admitted to official kindergartens maintained by the municipalities from the age of five, while in other cantons they may be admitted to private kindergartens at two; sometimes the kindergarten is the product of a joint effort by private initiative and municipal authorities, while in other cases the canton has taken the place of the local authorities and set up official playschools, which usually take children from the age of four. In all cases, attendance is optional and parents are free to send their children or not. Despite this great structural diversity, the demand for places is rising steadily. Recent statistics for all the Swiss cantons show that 93 per cent of pupils in the first year of compulsory schooling have spent one or more years in a kindergarten or playschool.

[. . .]

Convinced of the importance of the infant stage in the child's development, and believing that Switzerland could do still more towards overcoming the problems of young children, the cantons which have signed the concordat, acting through their executive body, the Conference of Cantonal Directors of Public Education, set up, in autumn 1980, an 'early childhood' working group to study not only from the educational point of view but also in terms of health and what is commonly called child-care, the problems connected with the child's development from birth to the age of eight, and to work in a spirit of coordination and cooperation.

[. . .]

TURKEY

[. . .]

It is a commonly shared opinion that the most characteristic and remarkable feature of this century is the rapid social change that has been taking place, and which we are all experiencing.

We have to make sure that our children are educated so that they can adjust easily to the varying demands of contemporary life and also keep abreast of new developments as they occur.

We need to educate our children so that they become self confident, self-directing individuals who are able to help themselves, and at the same time contribute to the society in which they live. Only in this way, can we bring into existence a generation fit for a democratic society.

A major goal of education during early childhood is to help young children to think not simply of themselves but to develop a concern for the welfare of others and a knowledge of the social world that surrounds them.

If a government wishes to improve the educational services offered to children and to their families, it is essential that as much as possible should be known about the environment in which the child grows up. Pre-school education during these critical years of rapid development is one way of ensuring greater equality of opportunity among children of different backgrounds. Pre-school education can provide rich environmental stimuli for those children coming from different social and economic backgrounds.

The fundamental changes of attitudes within any family towards the children depend very much on the social and economic level of the region and of the family, on the educational level of the parents and on differences in the number of children in the family.

We believe that formal education as well as non-formal education will play a great part in the solution of the problem which we are discussing. Until the time comes when formal pre-school facilities are fully developed, we can approach the problem found in developing countries, by ensuring that pre-school education is given to children within the family. In order to achieve this, we have to educate parents through adult education courses, through mass-media, through mobile teams of social workers, and so on.

Parents should be actively involved in the planning and implementation of pre-school education. In this way, the attitudes we want children to acquire in school will be encouraged and reinforced in the home.

Where it is not possible to provide a formal educational service to all children of pre-school age, one solution may be to lower the age of compulsory primary school attendance by one year. In this first pre-primary class, we can then plan our programme in terms of the principles of pre-school education, and in this way provide a smooth transition to primary education. In Turkey, we are carrying out studies along these lines.

We are convinced that in order to ensure a smooth transition from pre-school to primary education, teachers at both levels should be made familiar with the goals and techniques appropriate to both pre-school and primary levels.

Finally, let me raise a matter that is of great concern to us in Turkey. We feel it is most important for children of migrant workers to benefit from the pre-school education facilities in their host countries, so that these children can begin their basic education well-prepared, and on an equal footing, with native-born children. We are most anxious that all the countries concerned give this matter proper and serious consideration.

UNITED KINGDOM

[. . .]

In the UK, we have an earlier start to formal education than in most other countries in the world, and children can start school before they reach compulsory school age. Indeed, 56 per cent of all four year olds in the UK are receiving education. Moreover, the education service in the United Kingdom is not centrally controlled. There are four different education departments in the UK. Although it is a national service, it is locally administered, and for children of below compulsory school age, local education authorities have discretion in the form and amount of educational provision to be made.

The third point is that education for children of this age in the UK is not a child-minding service designed to enable parents to go out to work: it is mainly directed to meeting the needs of the child, though in doing so, it is intended to take family circumstances into account.

We have, of course, like other countries, a parallel social service, which is concerned with the family as a whole and it is important to realize that the social services also, when they deal with pre-school age children, are primarily concerned with what is best for the child.

In the UK the four education departments adopted a policy in 1972 of expanding nursery education to make it available for all children whose parents wanted them to have it. Unfortunately, the economic situation deteriorated for most of us in the mid-Seventies and neither the national government nor local education authorities in the United Kingdom have been able to make sufficient resources available to increase nursery education as quickly as we all would have wished. But progress has certainly been made.

In January 1980, 43 per cent of three and four year olds in the United Kingdom were receiving nursery education, compared with 17 per cent ten years earlier: and if we count also the four year olds who are attending primary schools, as well as those in nursery education, then the figure in 1980 was 56 per cent of all four year olds.

It is an important point in the UK that all our teachers must be qualified, and that this includes teachers of children who are below compulsory school age. It applies to nursery schools just as much as to primary schools. A nursery teacher today takes a three or four year course of training leading to a qualification for teaching children in the three-to-seven age group.

We believe it is vital that children beginning their education should be under the control of teachers specially trained to recognize their needs. In nursery education classes, there is also usually a second adult, who will have taken a two year course of training in child care, who works with the children under the direction of the teacher.

In our schools, this gives us an adult:pupil ratio of about 1:13. We think this is important for children of three and four, and it is one of the reasons why we think nursery education has advantages over early admission to primary schools. We also believe that our part-time nursery education pattern is the right way to start children on their education.

But high adult:pupil ratios produce high running costs, and it would be unrealistic in these times to expect to be able to increase nursery education provision substantially. However provision is being increased gradually year by year, and it is a cause for satisfaction that its value is now so well recognized that local authorities have not been tempted to reduce it, when they have been asked by the government to make cuts in their expenditure. Indeed, the number of children attending nursery classes in England increased by 5,600 between 1979, when the present government came to power, and 1980. The accommodation for this expansion has been largely achieved by the conversion to nursery education use of surplus primary school classrooms, which are a consequence of falling primary school rolls.

As long as nursery education is not available to everybody, there has to be a degree of selection to decide which children should be admitted. The policy of successive governments since 1968 has been to give special help to inner city and urban areas by specific grants, and now 70 per cent of nursery education is provided in those areas. It is, of course, difficult to strike a balance between rural and urban areas, and this is a problem that concerns us all. In the UK we have attempted to attain an even distribution of resources by a formula agreed with the local authority associates. It is, of course, unlikely that any local authority would be able to provide the same proportion of provision in sparsely-populated areas as in the inner cities; nevertheless, Devon, an authority which has to administer a large rural population, is attempting to provide nursery education for as many children as possible by arranging for a teacher and nursery assistant to travel to different parts of the county on different days.

Decisions on admission to nursery education are generally left to the head teacher, who gives priority to children with special needs. Children with poor language development, whether because of neglect by their parents or because their first language is not English, will be given priority, as will children who are handicapped or who are disadvantaged in some other way. Very often social services will draw the attention of a teacher to a child who could benefit from nursery education. Indeed, all support services for the under-fives, including health, have an important role to play in the development of all children.

The policy of ensuring that children with the greatest need are given priority will be further developed as a result of new legislation currently before our Parliament which is designed to reform the legal framework governing the provision of special education. This legislation, which we hope will come into force in the autumn of 1982, places great stress on the early identification of children with special needs. Parents who are worried about their child's development at any age from birth onwards will be given the right to request an assessment of their child's special educational needs, and local education authorities will be enabled to make appropriate measures to meet those needs.

From the age of two onwards, the local education authorities will be placed under a duty to identify those children with severe or complex learning difficulties, arising from any cause, and having assessed those needs and recorded them in a statement, to make suitable educational arrangements for that child. Throughout the whole process of identification, assessment, and decisions on the appropriate form of education to meet individual children's special needs, the legislation places great stress on the involvement of parents, and parents will be given absolute rights to consultation at different stages in the procedures.

Our latest Education Act contains a section which requires there to be at least two parent governors on the governing body of every primary or secondary school, and encourages the same for our nursery schools. Since most nursery education is in nursery classes attached to primary schools, parents are effectively brought into the governing arrangements. I am glad to say that, increasingly, parents are being encouraged to enter and help in the nursery school and nursery class. But we are anxious that nursery schools and classes should support the efforts of parents, not supplant them. We take the line that the parent is the first and most important educator of the child.

Education does not, of course, exist in a vacuum. Teachers must work with those in other services — health, social services, and voluntary services. We believe coordination between them in what they do for the under-fives is vital, if the total needs of the children are to be met, and we are to get good value for money. The central government departments responsible for under-fives work closely together and assist coordination wherever possible. One example is in the Education Act 1980, which allows local education authorities to make nursery teachers available to children in local authority day nurseries, so as to help children whose family circumstances are such that they have to spend all day in a day nursery. It is hoped that by introducing teachers, it will be possible to give the children education they would not otherwise have received.

We also believe strongly in voluntary efforts in the community, and we welcome cooperation, for instance, between playgroup leaders and head teachers in nursery and primary schools. Where there are extra primary school places which cannot be used for nursery education, some head teachers allow the rooms to be used by playgroups run by parents for their children. Contacts of this kind can lead to the start of a good relationship between parents and teachers.

Statement on the Education of Three-to-Eight Year Olds

The European Ministers of Education, at the Twelfth Session of the Standing Conference, adopted the following Statement.

1 The value of pre-school education

1.1   The period from three-to-eight years of age is decisive in the development of all children. It is the most active phase of their awakening to the world about them and to their culture. It is a stage of rapid learning about social behaviour and relationships. It is also generally the period during which children acquire the basic skills of linguistic communication and numeracy which are essential to a normal, fruitful existence in modern society. Equality of opportunity and possibilities of self-expression, of self-determination and of playing a meaningful role later on in society depend to a large extent on the 'education' − in the widest sense of the term− received in early childhood. It is consequently the duty of parents and society as a whole to ensure such education within and outside the school with the utmost care.

1.2   Pre-school facilities have an undeniable part to play in the harmonious development of children themselves, besides providing an important service to society as care centres for the children of parents working outside the home. Without detracting from the natural role of the parents in the child's education, pre-school facilities provide for many infants a unique opportunity for meeting and learning from other children and adults, for obtaining new social and cultural experience as a useful preparation for future schooling, as well as contributing to their physical, mental and emotional development. In many cases pre-school can further provide some 'natural adjustment' for children with a physical or cultural handicap. It can also enable children of migrants to become acquainted with social and cultural conditions in the host country before compulsory schooling.

1.3 In most of our modern communities we have produced physical and social conditions (small nuclear families, or one-parent families, and discrete urban housing units, surrounded by cars and other physical dangers), in which the child growing up without the stimulus of the outside contacts available through pre-school institutions could be at risk of serious social and intellectual deprivation. In these circumstances it is essential for pre-school facilities to be given adequate support and to be developed as rapidly as possible to the point where they are available to all children.

1.4 Pre-school education, for both social and educational reasons, has developed in such a way that (however it is organized), it has become an accepted part of parents' expectations for children below compulsory school age. Given this development, education policy in relation to the pre-school sector now needs to be reviewed in conjunction with the first years of primary schooling and all other aspects of policy which affect − overtly or indirectly − young children and their families.

1.5 It is therefore appropriate, in the light of the varied experience gathered in Europe, for this Standing Conference to examine the specific role of pre-school education and its interaction with compulsory school education. While this evidently differs from country to country according to the nature and extent of the pre-school provision, and the age of starting compulsory school, consideration of each type of system in use can demonstrate both risks and opportunities of relevance to all. The general principles of good education for this age group have been identified by research and incorporated in policy statements; the practical solutions in operation do not yet however always relate to these principles and policies.

2 Pre-school for all

2.1 Most countries intend maintaining pre-school provision on a non-compulsory basis given that a very high percentage of children

attend where facilities exist. However, in some countries pre-school
education is extensive and provided for in national legislation; in
some of these countries the question is being posed whether it
should not be extended to all children, and eventually, when a
situation is reached where a high percentage (90 per cent or over) of
the relevant age group participate, whether it should not be made
compulsory, that is, by gradual lowering of the age at which compulsory school starts. In some countries legislation to this end is
being initiated. Such a development would have as one of its aims
the protection of the remaining small percentage (often including
those most in need of pre-school education), who would otherwise
be at a disadvantage in starting primary school without experience
of pre-school education. Systems of this type present opportunities
to eliminate problems of transition betwen 'pre-school' and school
by integration of the pre-school sector within the school system.

2.2   On the other hand, in all countries pre-school education is too
valuable in its own right to be allowed to become merely an extension downwards of present school provision; any risk of development in that direction should be circumvented by appropriate policy
measures to retain the emphasis in the pre-school stage on social and
individual (physical and cultural) development, and in addition, to
encourage the extension of the creativity of the best practice in pre-
school classes further into the primary school. In countries where
pre-school education is not widespread and/or where pre-school and
primary education are not integrated, this aim may be achieved by
retaining the voluntary basis of pre-school education but integrating
into the system special support services for those most in need of
pre-school education.

2.3   In terms of the relationship between the school and the family or
local community, centralized and generalized pre-school systems can
provide flexibility in meeting local needs and responsiveness to
parents' desire for involvement. However, both in such systems and
in primary schools in general distinct efforts must be made to
achieve active participation by parents and other adults concerned in
order to mobilize the maximum possible resources in the educational
process and give parents an opportunity to interact with, and learn
from, the school. Above all, however, active parental participation
must be advocated in the interests of the child to create the optimal
environment for the development of his learning possibilities. The
actual right of parents to participate in pre-school or school organi-

zations ought to be exercised through direct contact between parents and teachers. The various kinds of parents' groups, at each level, ought also to be encouraged by public authorities. In all cases attention should be paid to increasing parents' real and practical opportunities to contribute effectively to the process of the education of their children. The practical involvement of parents in providing learning experience for children may be the most useful form of participation.

3 Care and education

3.1 Large-scale provision for pre-school education is in some cases made under the responsibility of authorities other than Education Ministries. This underlines the necessity of coordination with the 'care' aspects of services for young children – both in terms of the link between day-care and pre-school and in terms of cooperation between educational and health/welfare services.

3.2 In such a system, however, particularly active measures need to be taken to ensure coordination – but not uniformity – of the pedagogical content and methods of the earlier provision with the teaching of the first stages of primary school. The staff of nursery centres and of primary schools should be trained in such a way that consistency of the goals and continuity of the practice between the two sectors becomes a reality.

4 Community-based provision

4.1 Where pre-school facilities are organized by local authorities, parents or volunteers, opportunities naturally exist for responsiveness to the needs of the local community and for the active involvement of parents. If there is no large-scale provision or standardization of facilities, however, problems may occur in the transition to primary school, since children will arrive there with widely differing experience and those without pre-schooling may be at a disadvantage in terms of social competence.

4.2 It may also be more difficult in such a system to set up institutional links to help overcome problems in the transition to primary school. This situation therefore calls for particular attention to be given to the educational content and methods of primary classes, as well as to their size; the school should arrange its activities to suit children having different ranges of experience and should use this potential as an added educational resource.

5 Essential features for development

5.1 In States with pre-school systems as yet less developed but growing rapidly, choices can be made between the different possible types of structure and their attendant advantages or dangers. The solutions which unified systems may present to certain of the problems have to be weighed against considerations of adaptability and of cost. Whatever the setting, however, the following features can be identified as desirable:

i) use of play, music, art and other activities to develop social abilities, communication, creativity, self-expression and physical fitness and to stimulate learning faculties;

ii) more opportunities for children of different social, racial and religious groups (including the handicapped to as great an extent as possible), to be educated together, in the interests of cultivating tolerance and open-mindedness from the earliest age;

iii) use of the opportunity at the pre-school stages to help children overcome possible cultural difficulties (linguistic problems in particular), as well as to enable migrant children to become acquainted with social and cultural conditions in the host country before entry to primary school. In this context the Conference further recommends study of the special measures which are provided in some countries to improve the performance of migrant children in their mother tongue so as to strengthen their own cultural identity;

iv) elimination, in pre-school and primary stages, of sex-stereotyping;

v) involvement of parents in the work of the school, as a necessary element in the creation (at home and at school), of an effective learning environment for the child, as an additional resource for the school and as a means of community education;

vi) provision of classes of a size which gives maximum opportunity for teacher/child interaction and the social development of the individual child according to his pace of advancement and particular abilities;

vii) coordination, through teacher-training (including in-service training), institutional cooperation and classroom practice, of the goals and methods of the pre-school and primary sectors of education in order, inter alia, to facilitate the transition between these two stages;

viii) compatibility of care and education hours with local work-hours, in order to enable parents to accompany their children to such facilities; encouragement of flexibility in the fixing of work-hours to give parents more time for their children without risk of discrimination in the labour market;

ix) responsiveness, wherever possible, to regional circumstances (for example, need for special transport facilities or for mobile visiting services for homes in mountainous or other sparsely-populated areas); use of the local environment as a learning resource.

6 Coordination with other policy areas

6.1 Pre-school education policy, including day-care policies, cannot be viewed in isolation from labour market, housing, family allowance and taxation policies.

6.2 Provision of generally accessible pre-school education (free or at low cost to parents), for all parents who want it for their children is the only adequate response to the level of demand currently in existence. It has to be recognized that this demand springs from awareness of the benefits of good pre-school education for the individual development of the child, as well as the desire or need of most adults to work, and changes in the pattern of women's expectations of their role and in the pattern of family structures. It should therefore be recognized in policy planning that the demand for pre-school education will continue to grow and that education provision for the three-to-eight year olds should be coordinated with other types of day-care facility. The goal of providing pre-school education for all who wish it for their children should be recognized as urgently requiring implementation both on grounds of its educational value and also as a necessary part of social policy.

7 From the extensive work carried out on pre-school education in the organizations contributing to the Standing Conference it can be seen that the benefits of international cooperation in an area where there is a great variation between national systems lie not necessarily in

attempting to work towards one unified system, but in using international comparison as an analytical tool to identify the advantages
and disadvantages of each system and to use this analysis in
improving the individual system.

8 In view of the need for more widespread provision of pre-school
education and of the present financial and economic situation, the
international organizations are invited to continue their study of
policies for pre-school education and the financial problems they
pose.

Appendix A

Text of the Declaration adopted by the Council of Europe Conference on *From birth to eight: young children in European society in the 1980s*
(Strasbourg, 17-20 December, 1979)
as amended and adopted by the Committee of Ministers on 23 January, 1981

Recommendation no. R (81) 3 of the Committee of Ministers to Member States concerning the Care and Education of Children from Birth to the Age of Eight[1]

The Committee of Ministers, under the terms of Article 15b of the Statute of the Council of Europe,

Considering that the aim of the Council of Europe is to achieve a greater unity between its members and that this aim is to be pursued, in particular, through common action in the social and cultural fields;

Bearing in mind the United Nations' Declaration on the Rights of the Child (1959);

Having regard to Recommendation 874 (1979) of the Assembly on a European Charter on the Rights of the Child;

Having regard to the Declaration on the care and education of the child from birth to eight adopted by the Conference on the theme 'From birth to eight: young children in European Society in the 1980s', which

---

[1] In accordance with Article 10.2(c) of the Rules of Procedure for the meetings of the Ministers' Deputies, the Representatives of Ireland and of the United Kingdom approved the adoption of this text but reserved the right of their governments to comply with it or not.

was organized by the Council for Cultural Cooperation in Strasbourg from 17-20 December 1979;

Recalling that this Conference was one of the Council of Europe contributions to the International Year of the Child (1979);

Considering the importance of the care and education of children from birth to eight;

Recommends that the governments of member States:

a) take account, in their policies on the care and education of young children, of the principles set out in Section I of the Appendix hereto and take measures concerning their implementation set out in Section II of the Appendix;

b) ensure that this Recommendation is distributed as widely as possible among interested persons and bodies.

Appendix to Recommendation No. R (81) 3

I   Principles concerning the Care and Education of the Child from Birth to Eight

THE RIGHTS OF THE CHILD

The child must enjoy the fundamental rights as set out in the United Nations Declaration on the Rights of the Child, as well as the right to develop his physical, emotional, intellectual, social and spiritual potential to the full and to be respected as an individual in his own right.

The child will normally depend primarily on his family to recognize and secure these rights. The family operates within a wider social framework from which it should be able to obtain the support it needs to fulfil its obligations. In providing such support, care should be taken not to undermine parental responsibilities towards the child.

All services with a contribution to make to the development of young children — especially health, education and social services — should work with, and through, the family to provide continuity of experience for the child.

THE CARE AND EDUCATION OF YOUNG CHILDREN

The care and education of pre-school children should fulfil the following criteria. They should:

meet the child's need for security and affection and social life, including leisure activities, with other children and adults; provide the conditions for good physical and mental health; stimulate the child's creative and intellectual development and his capacity for expression; help the child to become integrated in his environment and cope with life, and encourage the child's independence, initiative and free play; respect the child's cultural and psychological identity and recognize his uniqueness and individuality; open up both family and pre-school circles to the wider society to enable the child to meet other people of all ages.

Educational provision should be made available for all children whose parents wish them to have it during at least two years preceding the start of primary school. The lack of financial means should not be a barrier to children who need such educational provision.

Support services — including health, social services and education — have an important role to play in the development of all children, but the form of provision should take account of their particular needs, which differ according to their stage of development, their personal capacities and their cultural backgrounds:

children who live in urban areas have great need of care and education owing to living conditions in towns: lack of space, pollution of various kinds, dangers in the streets, parents' absence (time spent at work plus travelling time);

children who live in rural and sparsely populated areas are more difficult to cater for. It is therefore necessary to find untraditional and flexible solutions to bring pre-school education to these children;

children who live in circumstances of extreme socioeconomic deprivation have special needs;

children of cultural minorities, whether native or immigrant, should receive an education which promotes their integration into the regional or national community, as a basis for mutual enrichment;

handicapped children should, whenever necessary, have available to them establishments which meet their special needs.

In association with child care and child psychological services, health services should operate within pre-school care and education provision to detect, assess and treat handicapping conditions.

PEOPLE AND AGENCIES PARTICIPATING IN THE CARE AND
EDUCATION OF YOUNG CHILDREN
All those contributing to the care and education of young children
(including the family in the widest sense, the community and self-help
groups, volunteers, teachers), should be able to benefit from the
findings of up-to-date research and knowledge of developments in the
concept of early education and, whenever appropriate, to participate in
such research.

Professionals need initial training supplemented by in-service
training. Both should be of the highest possible quality.

II   Role of Member States

Taking into account the importance of care and education of children
from birth to eight in European society in the 1980s, member States
should:

1 organize the care and education of young children, in close cooperation with parents, as a means of complementing family upbringing
   and as a first stage in life-long learning. This should be done by:
      providing adequate funds,
      improving family, social and labour legislation,
      planning education systems in such a way as to maintain conti-
      nuity and to educate children to become creative and innovatory
      adults;
2 prepare parents and future parents for the responsibilities inherent
   in the education of young children;
3 assume responsibility or provide support for organizations and
   institutions caring for young children, especially for those children
   whose need is most obvious;
4 promote and encourage research and the training of staff in order to
   provide children with care and education, under the best possible
   conditions, supervised by highly qualified staff, who, as far as
   possible, should operate in multidisciplinary teams;
5 ensure that the various national, regional and local administrations
   coordinate family and child care services to guarantee continuity of
   experience for the child.

Appendix B

List of those who have contributed to the compiling of this report

1 Members of the Working Party set up by the Committee of Senior Officials

Professor Maria Helena AMORIM, Department of Science and Education, University of Aveiro (Portugal)
Mrs Agnete ENGBERG, Directorate of Primary and Lower Secondary Education, Ministry of Education (Denmark)
Mr L. VAN DER GAAG, Director, Ministry of Education and Science (Netherlands)
Mr Hans-Erik ÖSTLAND, Head of Planning and Budget Secretariat, Ministry of Education (Sweden)
Mr Roland ROOSE, Secretaris Generaal, Ministerie van Nationale Opvoeding en Nederlandse Cultuur (Belgium)
Mrs Maria da Graça TEIXEIRA, Inspector of Pre-School Education, Ministry of Education (Portugal)
Mr Maitland STOBART, Head of School Education Division, Directorate of Education, Culture and Sport (Council of Europe)
Mr Norberto BOTTANI, Head of the Project 'Early Childhood Education' (OECD/CERI)
Miss Ida SUBARAN, Programme specialist, Education Sector (UNESCO)
Mr Patrick DAUNT, Principal Administrator, Directorate for Education and Training, Directorate General for Employment and Social Affairs – Education – (Commission of the European Communities)

2 National Liaison Officers

Austria	Dr Dieter ANTONI, Oberkommisär, Zentrum für Schulversuche und Schulentwicklung
Belgium	Mr L. POLLENTIER, Inspecteur général, Ministère de l'Education Nationale et de la Culture Néerlandaise
Cyprus	Miss Leto PAPACHRISTOFOROU, Primary School Inspector, Ministry of Education
Denmark	Mrs Jytte HOLMES, Economy and Statistics Division, Ministry of Education
Finland	Department for International Relations, Ministry of Education
France	M. Daniel CHAILLET, Inspecteur dAcadémie, Chargé de Mission auprès due Directeur des Ecoles, Service des Affaires Internationales, Secrétariat d'Etat, Ministère de l'Education
Germany	Ltd. Ministerialrätin Dr TUMBRÄGEL, Ministerium für Gesundheit, Soziales und Sport des Landes Rheinland-Pflaz
	Regierungsdirektor Dr Horst ROCHE, Sekretariat der Ständigen Konferenz der Kultusminister der Länder
Greece	Mr A. PROVATARES, Director of Implementation of Primary and Pre-School Curricula, Ministry of Education
Holy See	Père Francisco MIGOYA, S.J., Congrégation pour l'Education Catholique
Ireland	Miss Eleanor O'BRIEN, Department of Education
Italy	Professor Corrado CANDIDI, Inspecteur central, Ecole primaire
Liechtenstein	Dr Josef WOLF, Schulamt, Landesverwaltung
Luxembourg	M. Henri HOSTERT, Conseiller de Gouvernement, Ministère de l'Education Nationale
Malta	Mr J. Zammit MANGION, c/o Education Office
Netherlands	Mrs J. BRUINING, Ministry of Education and Science
Norway	Mr Per MILJETEIG-OLSSEN, Ministry of Consumer Affairs and Public Administration
Portugal	Mrs Darnell NOBREGA, Ministry of Education
Spain	Mrs Clara DEL ARCO, Chef du Cabinet de l'Enseignement Préscolaire, Ministère de l'Education

Sweden   Mr Hans-Erik ÖSTLUND, Head of Planning and
                Budget Secretariat, Ministry of Education
Switzerland   Professor Eugène EGGER, Secrétaire Général de la
                Conférence suisse des Directeurs cantonaux de
                l'Instruction publique
Turkey   Direction Générale des Relations Extérieures,
                Ministère de l'Education Nationale
United Kingdom Mr E.B. GRANSHAW, Schools Branch 1, Department
                of Education and Science.

*3 Secretariat of the Standing Conference of European Ministers of
Education*

Ms Joan F. DAVIDSON, Administrator, Directorate of Education,
Culture and Sport, Council of Europe
Mrs Katia WEIL, Directorate of Education, Culture and Sport,
Council of Europe

References

ANDREOLO, R. (1977). 'Cooperation between parents, pre-school and the community'. The 'Organi Collegiali' in Italy. Strasbourg: Council of Europe. CCC/EGT (77) 6.

ASKLING, B. (1979). *Training of pre-school teachers in Sweden: current structures and some development trends.* Stockholm: Swedish Institute.

BADINTER, E. (1981). *The Myth of Motherhood.* London: Souvenir Press.

BONE, M. (1977). *Pre-school children and their needs for day care.* London: HMSO.

BRADSHAW, J. and PIACHAUD, D. (1980). *Child Support in the European Community.* Occasional Papers in Social Administration. London: Bedford Square Press.

BRONFENBRENNER, U. (1974). *Two Worlds of Childhood.* Harmondsworth: Penguin.

CEBEON, B.Y. (1979). *Onderzoek naar effecten aktivering innovatie basisonderwijs.* Amsterdam.

COLLIS, G.M. and SCHAFFER, H.R. (1975) 'Synchronisation of visual attention in mother-infant pairs', *Jnl. Child Psych. and Psychiatr.,* 16, pp. 315-20.

COMMISSION OF THE EUROPEAN COMMUNITIES (1979). *The Europeans and their Children.* Brussels: EEC.

CONDRY, G. (1980). *Diploma in Early Childhood Studies.* London: Roehampton Institute.

CORBETT, A. (1980). 'New Styles in Training of Professionals and Parents'. In: OECD. *Children and Society: Issues for Pre-School Reforms.* Paris: CERI.

CORDEN, A., PIACHAUD, D. and BRADSHAW, J. (1980). 'How Europe meets family costs', *New Society,* Oct. 23, pp. 159-61.

COUNCIL OF EUROPE (1973). *The training of teaching staff engaged in pre-school education.* DECS/EGT (73) 22. Strasbourg.

COUNCIL OF EUROPE (1979). *Priorities in pre-school education.* Strasbourg.

DAS, J.P. (1979). *Cognitive processes in children: consideration for a cross-national perspective.* Paris: UNESCO.

DAVIE, R., BUTLER, N. and GOLDSTEIN, H. (1972). *From Birth to Seven.* London: Longman.

DE BLOCK, A., *et al.* (1980). *Samenvatting van her voorlopig en partieel evaluatie-rapport betreffende het VLO-Project.* University of Ghent.

DEPARTMENT OF EDUCATION AND SCIENCE (ENGLAND AND WALES). (1975). *A Language for Life.* (The Bullock Report). London: HMSO.

DEPARTMENT OF EDUCATION AND SCIENCE (ENGLAND AND WALES). (1978). *Primary Education in England: a survey by HM Inspectors of schools.* London: HMSO.

DE WITT, S. (1977). 'Links between pre-school and primary education'. Lecture to the Council of Europe Bournemouth seminar. Roneoed.

FERRI, E. (1980). 'Combined nursery centres', Concern, No. 37, pp. 6-11. London: National Children's Bureau.

GOODNOW, J. (1979). 'Child Development'. In: *Social Security, IYC* Edition, Canberra, Australia.

GOUTARD, M. (1980). *Pre-school Education in the European Community.* Commission of the European Communities. Ed. Series No. 12. Brussels.

INNOVATIE COMMISSIE OPLEIDINGEN BASISONDERWIJS. (1980). *The structure of teacher education for the basisonderwijs* (trans). The Hague: Ministry of Education.

JANSSEN-VOS, F. (1977). 'Contacten met ouders: bijzaak of noodzaak', Amsterdam: *Jeugd in School en Wereld.*

KAMERMAN, S. and KAHN, A.J. (1980). *Child-care, Family Benefits and Working Parents: a study in comparative policy.* New York: Columbia University School of Social Work.

KONOPKA, G. (1979). 'IYC, with emphasis on the concern for adolescents'. In: *Social Security, IYC* Edition, Canberra, Australia.

LAWRENCE, D. and BLAGG, N. (1974). 'Improved reading through self-initiated learning and counselling', *Remedial Education, 9, 7.*

LAZAR, I. and DARLINGTON, R.B. (1978). *Lasting Effects after Pre-school.* A report of the Consortium for Longitudinal Studies. Ithaca, New York: Cornell University.

LE BRAS, H. (1979). *Child and Family.* Paris: OECD.

LILJESTROM, R. (1980). *Children and Culture.* Cultural Policy Studies, Series No. 1. Strasbourg: Council of Europe.

LJUNGBLAD, T. (1979). 'Pre-school and primary school in cooper-ation'. Department of Educational Research. University of Gothenborg.
LÜSCHER, K. (1980). In: OECD. *Children and Society: Issues for Pre-school Reforms.* Paris: CERI.
LURCAT, L. (1979). *The Needs and Rights of Children.* Strasbourg: Council of Europe.

MANTOVANI, S. (1978). 'Current trends in Italian pre-school policy', *Int. Jnl. of Behavioural Devel.*, 1.
MARIET, F. (1980). *Maintaining migrants' links with the culture of their countries of origin.* Strasbourg: Council of Europe. DECS/EGT (79) 77; RS-LC (79) 1.
MINISTRY OF EDUCATION, NETHERLANDS. (1980). *The primary school innovation process in the Netherlands.* The Hague: Depart-mental Project Group.
MINISTRY OF EDUCATION, FRANCE. (1975). *Scolarisation en maternelle et scolarité primaire: le cas de l'arrondissement de Valenciennes.* Lille: CRDP.
MISITI, R. (1979). *The Needs of the Young Child.* Strasbourg: Council of Europe.

NEWSON, E. and J. (1968). *Four Year Olds in an Urban Community.* London: George Allen & Unwin.
NEWSON, E. and J. (1976). *Seven Year Olds in the Home Environ-ment.* London: George Allen & Unwin.
NORA, S. and MINC, A. (1980). *The Computerisation of Society.* Cambridge, Mass: MIT Press.

OECD (1978). *Pre-school Education: reports from five research projects.* Paris.
OECD (1980). *Policies for Children: Analytical Report.* Paris: CERI, ECE/80.02.

PLOWDEN REPORT, GREAT BRITAIN, DEPARTMENT OF EDU-CATION AND SCIENCE. Central Advisory Council for Education (England) (1967). *Children and their Primary Schools.* London: HMSO.
PLUMB, J.H. (1975). *The New World of Children in Eighteenth Century England.* Past & Present. London.
PSACHAROPOULOS, G. (1980). *The Economics of Early Childhood Services.* CERI/ECE/80.03. Paris: OECD.

RAVEN, J. (1981). *Early Intervention − a selective review of the literature.* Edinburgh: Scottish Council for Research in Education.

SADLI, S. (1979). *Changing Patterns of Child-Rearing Practices: an Indonesian Study.* Paris: UNESCO.

SANDGREN, B. (1980). 'Integration between the educational sector and the health and welfare sector within the policies for children'. In: OECD. *Children and Society: Issues for Pre-School Reforms.* Paris: CERI.

SCHEFFKNECHT, J.J. (1978). *European network of inter-action projects in adult education.* Strasbourg: Council of Europe. DECS/EES (78) 55.

SIJELMASSI, M. (1979). *Certain cultural and social aspects of children in some Arab countries.* Paris: UNESCO.

SINGER, E. (1980). 'Women, children and child-care centres'. In: OECD. *Children and Society: Issues for Pre-School Reforms.* Paris: CERI.

SHORTER, E. (1976). *The Making of the Modern Family.* London: Collins.

STRATHCLYDE EXPERIMENT IN EDUCATION (1977). *The Govan Project: Interim Report.* Department of Education, University of Glasgow.

STUDY COMMISSION ON THE FAMILY (1980). *Happy Families?* A discussion paper on families in Britain. London.

TIZARD, J., HEWISON, J. and SCHOFIELD, W.N. (1980). *The Haringey Reading Project.* London: Thomas Coram Research Unit.

TIZARD, J. (Ed.) (1980). *Children and Society: Issues for Pre-School Reforms.* Paris: OECD/CERI.

TIZARD, J. and MANTOVANI, S. (1980). 'Day Care Problems'. In: OECD. *Children and Society: Issues for Pre-School Reforms.* Paris: CERI.

TOMLINSON, J. (1977). *Cooperation between parents, pre-school and the community.* The Children's House, Crewe (United Kingdom). Strasbourg: Council of Europe. CCC/EGT (77) 3.

UNESCO. (1979). *Wastage in primary education: a statistical study of trends and patterns in repetition and drop-out.* ED/BIE/37/Ref. 2. Paris.

VAN DER EYKEN, W., BUTLER, N. and OSBORN, A. (1982). (in preparation). *Pre-Schooling in Britain.* University of Bristol.

VITTACHI, A. (1979). 'Let's Make it Two', *New Internationalist,* 79, Sept.

WEISS, J., REIN, M. and WHITE, S. (1980). 'The Plea for Coordination of Services for Young Children'. In: OECD. *Children and Soceity: Issues for Pre-School Reforms.* Paris: CERI.

WOLFSON, J. (1980). 'Parent Education: The Open University Experience'. In: OECD. *Children and Society: Issues for Pre-School Reforms.* Paris: CERI.

WOODHEAD, M. (1977). *Cooperation between Parents, Pre-School and the Community.* Strasbourg: Council of Europe.

WOODHEAD, M. (1979). *Pre-School Education in Western Europe: Issues, Policies and Trends.* Council of Europe. London: Longman.

WORSLEY, P. (ed). (1977). 'The Family in Industrial Society'. In: *Introducing Sociology.* 2nd edition. Harmondsworth: Penguin.

WYNN, M. and WYNN, W. (1979). *Some developments in child health care in Europe.* Eastbourne, England: Royal Society of Health Congress.